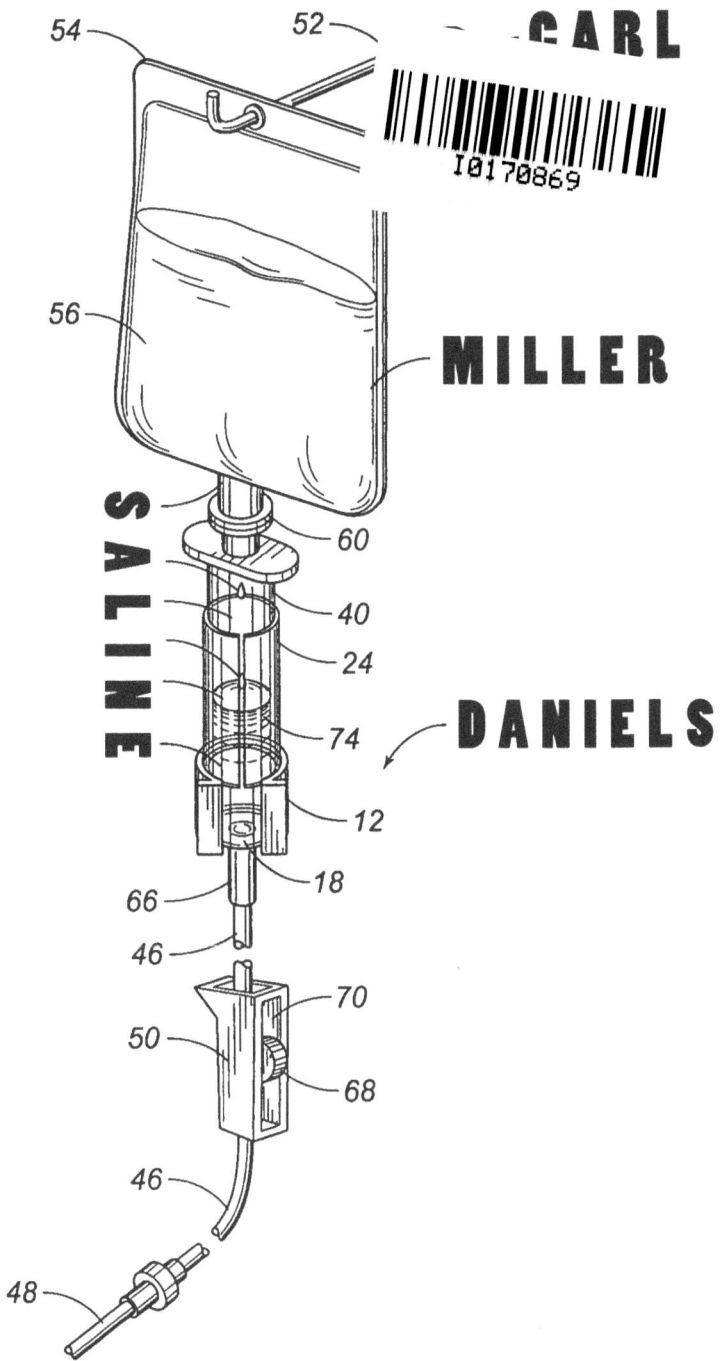

INTERIOR NOISE PRESS
Austin, TX

For order information and current mailing address please visit www.interiornoisepress.com

Interior Noise Press
Austin, TX

Cover Photograph by Carl Miller Daniels
Book Design by David p Bates

Library of Congress Control Number: 2014955492
ISBN: 978-0-9816606-4-6

First Edition

Dedicated to Jon
(aka "the sweetest man in the world")

CONTENTS

All the really good ideas I
ever had came to me while
I was milking a cow.

GRANT WOOD

saline

"green peppers and pickles can be remarkably satisfying,"
he thinks, sitting there in the screened-in porch,
the waves crashing onto the beach. he's wearing
only a towel, wrapped loosely around his waist.
sexy young and unkempt, he's discarded his
wet swimsuit, his legs
are spread, and he's enjoying the feel
of the sea breeze on his balls.
he's picking up slices of green pepper and
little green cucumber pickles from
a plate that's sitting in the middle
of the table. he's chewing the pepper slices
and the little cucumber pickles
slowly and methodically, and swallowing
them with great enthusiasm. some people
eat fish and shrimp and oysters and
scallops and things of this nature
while at the beach, but not him. never.
bits of vegetation is what he craves.
bits of vegetation is what he wants.
so he sits there, his legs spread,
the towel loosely draped, the
sea breeze on his balls, a mouthful
of sliced green peppers— and
the fish that frolic in the waves,
the crabs that pick at bits of
mysterious debris, the oysters and
scallops filtering the water for
mightily nutritious bits of floating
algae, are safe from him.
he yawns and stretches
and when the towel parts
to reveal his smooth pink
genitalia in a totally calm
and relaxed state of non-arousal,
his lips smack just a bit,

and the sea breeze feels
so wonderful, a whole
well-spring of emotion
best described as "elevation"
forms in his chest, and
he just goes on chewing,
crunch crunch crunch.

not all who wander are lost

i'm constantly revising the movie
BLUE LAGOON in my mind.
there's no brooke shields in my movie. there's
only me and christopher atkins, both of us running
around naked and having sex all the time.
i don't know if you've ever seen BLUE LAGOON or not,
but in that movie christopher atkins is a
beautiful blonde big-dicked
teenage boy. he was wide shoulders. tiny nipples.
a rippled belly. he is astonishingly hot. his voice
is sweet and gently masculine. he is yummy.
in BLUE LAGOON he and brooke shields are
trapped as children on a tropical island
after a ship wreck. they are the only
people on the island. no adults.
gradually, as they grow into teenagers,
they discover sex and have a baby.
but, in my constant revisions, there
is NO BROOKE SHIELDS on that island.
it's just me and christopher atkins.
one day while we're wrestling, our
dicks get hard and he discovers
he can butt-fuck me. we both
like it, and i discover that i can
butt-fuck him. we both like it.
we go for long swims in the warm
ocean, wash ourselves squeaky
clean, watch each other jerk off,
jerk each other off, suck each
other off, sleep together as one tangled
mass of hot moist teenage-boy flesh.
i love the smell of his sun-crinkled
blonde hair. the blue of his eyes.
the sexy manliness of his gentle
voice. as a teenage
boy, i am almost as good-looking

as he is. but let's face it: no one
is as good-looking as
christopher atkins. look him
up on google if you don't
believe me.
you'll see. and as to
those constant revisions i'm doing,
how does
christopher atkins butt-fuck my
tight little teenage-boy asshole?
wouldn't some kind of lubricant
be helpful? i mean, i'm just
a teenage boy, and my
asshole is really really TIGHT.
ah, coconut oil. coconuts
are plentiful on the island,
and we already know how
to get into them. that slick
slimy rind, run your fingers
over it, and they come out
slippery, feeling oily. just spread
it in the appropriate places, his
dick and my tight little pink asshole,
and my being butt-fucked
by christopher atkins
is almost easy. and, with
that stuff on my dick and
rubbed into his asshole,
i'm sure he'd feel
just about the same.
you can lick that stuff,
too, leaves your tongue
kinda mucky and oily.
christopher and i talk
about that flavor, and
he likes the smell
of my armpits as

much as i like the smell
of his armpits, which is
a lot, the sweaty wisps
of hair, his face against
my chest in the middle
of a hot tropical night.
**

he's so beautiful—
a puff of air
inside a bag
of skin.

lotus blossoms in the spring

bradley was driving.
matthew was sitting in the seat beside him.
everytime the car hit a pothole, matthew spurted
out a little teeny-tiny bit of cum.
whenever they hit a pothole, and matthew spurted out a little
teeny-tiny bit of cum, bradley laughed.
bradley was sexy, fully dressed, driving
in his usual manner, which was kind of fast,
and reasonably cautious.
matthew was sexy, outrageously handsome, and totally
naked. matthew had a big smooth hardon.
the car hit another pothole.
matthew spurted out a little teeny-tiny bit of cum.
bradley laughed, and pushed the accelerator
a little further toward the floor.
then bradley said: "hey, matthew, does it feel
good everytime you spurt a little bit of cum? does
it feel like a real orgasm?"
matthew, sitting there sexy naked and
big-dicked hard as a rock, said, "almost.
though it doesn't last as long as a regular orgasm,
of course. this one is just really really fast,
but real nice, too."
bradley purposefully steered the car
over a pothole. matthew spurted out
another teeny-tiny little bit of cum.
bradley laughed.
matthew blotted his own flat naked sexy belly
with a wadded up kleenex, and then tossed
it into the back of the car.
"and what kind of drug did you say you took
to get this reaction?" asked bradley,
guiding the car smoothly and carefully
through traffic.
"don't know," said matthew. "the guy
didn't tell me.

he just told me
what it'd do. so i thought,
what the heck... give it
a try..."
bradley, fully clothed,
driving the car, said,
"you total goof!"
"pretty much," said matthew.
matthew, totally naked, big smooth dick
nice and hard, smiled coquettishly.
bradley hit another pothole.
matthew spurted out another teeny-tiny bit of
cum.
both guys laughed like maniacs.
it was exactly that kind of day.

jeans and a t-shirt

as the words poured out of his mouth like
droplets of cum spurting out of his dick,
the sexy naked young man
told the guy who was jerking him off,
"god oh god that feels great i'm cumming
i'm cumming i'm spurting i'm hard
as a rock and i'm spurting cum and
spurting cum and spurting
more cum and spurting cum
feels incredibly incredibly goooood. god."
**

"my turn," says the guy who just
jerked off the first guy.
**

now, the guy who is getting jerked
off by the first guy, the talkative
guy, is the quiet type.
he just stands there while
the talkative guy jerks him
off from behind.
they both watch the whole procedure
in the big mirror on the back
of the bedroom door.
**

silent guy spurts cum.
silent guy spurts a LOT of cum.
**

after silent guy
spurts cum, talkative guy starts
talking again, and says, "i still
don't know why you don't want
me to say anything while i'm
jerking YOU off, especially
since you never say anything
yourself. don't you want
to talk about it? don't you

want to talk about how
incredibly good it feels
getting jerked off and
spurting cum?"
**

silent guy turns around
and looks at talkative guy.
silent guy says, "i like
my coffee black. you like
yours with lots of cream and
sugar. get it?"
**

talkative guy nods,
smiles. once again,
they are happy
in their relationship,
secure in their love.

a little more relish on that burger, please

the cute sexy big-dicked teenage boy pretended to be
in love with wanda jean.
but, in reality, the cute sexy big-dicked teenage boy
was in love with wanda jean's brother, ralph.
oh ralph was hot. oh ralph was smoldering.
oh ralph was ridiculously good-looking, and,
sometimes, when
the cute sexy big-dicked teenage boy
and wanda jean were making out on the couch,
ralph walked into the room, showing
off a big smooth hardon at the front of
his tight faded blue jeans.
the cute sexy big-dicked teenage boy
stared intently at ralph at these times.
ralph stared back at
the cute sexy big-dicked teenage boy, and
ralph's eyes kind of twinkled.
wanda jean pretended not to see
any of this, none of it, not a bit.
**

well, one day,
the cute sexy big-dicked teenage boy
showed up unexpected at wanda jean's house.
wanda jean was out shopping with her mom.
but her sexy brother ralph was home.
in fact, ralph was the only
one home.
ralph answered the door.
ralph was wearing only a towel, wrapped
loosely around
his waist. ralph looked wonderful.
ralph looked like sex on legs.
"come in," ralph said to
the cute sexy big-dicked teenage boy.
**

in no time at all,
ralph and the cute sexy big-dicked teenage boy

were up in ralph's bedroom,
naked, rolling around on the floor,
touching each and every part of each other
with quick eager fingers.
they spurted about 3 loads of cum, each,
before they got dressed
and went back into the living
room and sat there chatting innocently
when wanda jean and her mother walked in.
**

at one point in the conversation,
wanda jean and her brother ralph
exchanged weird, eerie, unsettling
kinds of glances. then, everybody
continued right along, talking pleasantly.
**

eventually the cute sexy big-dicked teenage boy
and wanda jean's brother ralph
moved into their own little apartment
and had sex for dozens of hours during
their very first week of living together.
the schedule continued pretty much
the same during subsequent weeks, as well.
those two just couldn't keep their hands
off of each other.
**

eventually,
wanda jean became very noble about the whole
thing. oh, for several months after
the cute sexy big-dicked teenage boy
and her brother
ralph
moved in together, she refused to
speak to either one of them.
but then, one night, they all
went out to dinner, had a good
laugh at the whole situation,

and, from then on,
everything was a-ok.
"fine as frog's hair," is a term
we have here in the South.
rivet.

hold your nose and close your eyes

for the most part, science is silent about
the existence of god. and so am i.
and i'm pretty sure that when i'm dead
and gone, i'll be competely and totally
gone. nothing to remain.
no soul. no ghost. none of that
there stuff.
it's just a hunch, of course, that
there will be nothing left of me.
but, well, it's a pretty strong hunch.
about the existence of god,
i've been an agnostic for a long
time, and don't really see that changing.
although i do lean more toward atheism
these days.
just a hunch.
**

right now, i'm pretty sure
there's a sexy naked big-dicked teenage boy
lying on his back on a big smooth rock
in the middle of the woods. there's
sunshine caressing his skin,
and, while the sunshine
caresses his skin, he
caresses his own big smooth purple-headed dick,
tugs gently on it, pats it,
rubs it,
urges it on as it gears up
to spurt several big gooey
gobs of hot mucusy cum.
so this sexy naked big-dicked teenage boy
lies there on that rock,
in total complete and abandoned bliss,
playing with his dick, soaking up
the rays of the sun,
and,

a gentle kaBOOM!
he starts spurting cum
and the electro-surge of orgasm
sparks from his dick to his balls,
to his nipples, to his toes,
to his throat, to his asshole,
to his earlobes, all in the
matter of just a few seconds.
**

years later,
many years later,
there's nothing left of him.
his dead body cremated.
dust in the wind.
it seems difficult to believe
that a sexy naked big-dicked teenage boy
jerking off hot and juicy in the woods
ends up that way.
nothing.
maybe a particle or two of dust might remain.
probably not, though.
just a hunch.

purchase order

"sunken treasure at the bottom of
the sea," thinks the
sexy naked big-dicked teenage boy.
"if only i could grow my fingers two
miles long, and just reach around
down there, and pull some of it
up."
the sexy naked big-dicked teenage boy
is used to watching something that
is one size, grow to a much bigger
size. so it doesn't seem like
too big a stretch of the imagination,
so to speak,
to imagine his own fingers growing and
growing and growing until
they are two miles long. sure, they
would be long and skinny
and scary-looking, but,
well, if they could feel around down
there and
then grab ahold
of some of that buried treasure
lurking at the bottom of the sea,
that would sure be nice.
the sexy naked big-dicked teenage boy
is standing on a secluded beach,
looking out to sea.
"it sure is pretty here," he thinks,
looking out to sea, and then
down, at his own big dick, expanding
now, to its full-on ready-to-spurt-cum
size.
like i said, he's used to seeing
at least one of his body parts
get longer, and longer, and
longer, and, as this happens now,

to his great big dick,
he looks at his fingers,
and at the bright
glossy shininess of the sea,
and
dream he does,
and dream
he does.

life on the theory of buckwheat

treating waterfalls with cyanide to control the
fish population is just wrong.
who does that?
someone i'm sure.
someone somewhere on this lovely
planet does that: treats waterfalls
with cyanide to control the fish
population.
what gets into people's heads anyway?
**

this, and other troubled thoughts,
are on the
mind of
the sexy naked big-dicked teenage boy
as he walks around inside his house.
his parents are gone.
he is an only child.
at this moment,
the sexy naked big-dicked teenage boy
would describe himself as "buck naked"
but he's heard other folks use the term
"butt naked" and he wonders which
is actually the correct term. but,
from what he knows of language,
he suspects that "buck naked" is
the proper term, and that it
has somehow been corrupted,
or modified, or idiomized,
to become "butt naked" which
is actually a tangier and earthier
term, charming in both its innocence
and in the hints of its ignorance.
the sexy naked big-dicked teenage boy
smiles. he likes words,
and he likes the way they
get slurried around, shuffled,

and reshuffled, and
wispified to the
tune of an evolutionary
imperative. everything
must change, mustn't it?
thinks the sexy naked big-dicked teenage boy
as he walks around "buck naked" inside
his house.
**

now, the sexy naked big-dicked teenage boy
is in his
bedroom, staring into his aquariums.
which word, he knows, can also be
"aquaria", due to its latin origins.
anyhow,
he licks his lips and smiles.
he likes his "fish tanks" (that
took care of that, didn't it!?), and,
as he watches his tropical
fish glide to and fro in
the crystal clear water,
he wonders how anyone
could put cyanide into
a waterfall.
to control the fish population.
the sexy naked big-dicked teenage boy
has sprouted a lovely hardon now,
and,
he tugs on it gently
as he stares at his
tropical fish
and the clear bubbling
water, when he gets
close to orgasm,
he lies down on
his back on top of
his bed and stares at

the ceiling. he tugs
on his dick some more
and soon, KA-BOOM!,
the orgasm begins
and he spurts cum
and spurts cum and
spurts yet more cum.
hot and gooey,
it coats his sexy naked chest
and his sexy naked belly.
and then,
it is over.
the sexy naked big-dicked teenage boy
lies there on his back,
his chest and belly drenched
with his own hot smelly
cum,
and the aquariums bubble,
and the fish swim to and fro.
"aquaria," thinks
the sexy naked big-dicked teenage boy.
"butt naked".
the word "semen". whence the
word "cum"?
and that word "jizz"?
the sexy naked big-dicked teenage boy
stands up and looks at himself
in the mirror. the warm goo
starts to dribble down his
chest and belly, toward the floor.
the sexy naked big-dicked teenage boy
looks good. anyone could see that
he looks good.
how good does he look?
and why does he know
he looks good? who taught him
to know that he looks good? who

taught us to know that he
looks good? and, for
that matter,
whence
the origins
of
desire?

cranberry punch marigold seeds

canterbury walk to the east of eden.
goldfish delight in christopher atkins.
the deep pockets of
persimmon breeders.
the sexy big-dicked teenage boy
who spurts his cum alone in the
middle of the night. sometimes
he's awake when the cum jets
out of him. sometimes he's
asleep.
the voices of old men,
after clearing the phlegm from
their throats.
old women singing in a church
choir. you want them to
sound so much better than they
actually do sound. they seem so eager to
please.
**

so in fact when the sexy big-dicked teenage boy
does wakes up, he does go ahead and wipe the
cum off of himself, and deposits his cum-soaked
underpants in the nearby laundry basket.
then, completely naked now, he stands looking at himself
in the big long mirror that runs the
entire length of his bedroom door.
the sexy naked big-dicked teenage boy looks
good. the sexy naked big-dicked teenage boy
knows he looks good, and he finds
it reassuring that he still looks good
even after soaking his underpants with
cum in the middle of the night.
the sexy naked big-dicked teenage boy
sort of remembers the dream he was
having when he spurted cum.
the bushy tails of squirrels.

hanging in thick rows from the
belt of jack, his best friend. suddenly,
no more squirrels' tails, and no
more belt. just jack, smiling,
something odd about jack's pubic
hair, though: is it gray now,
or purple?
**

sunrise finds the expletives
on the lips of even the most pious.
who wants to have to go to work
on a holiday? the ice is varnish
on the streets. the
banter of infants,
continually insipid.

tra la la

the circumstances under which i am in
bed with jamie bell are mysterious,
but, there we are, both naked,
and in bed together.
jamie bell is 26 years old now, and quite
sexy. i love his movies "billy elliot"
and "the chumscrubber" and "mr foe"
and "the eagle". he is incredibly
sexy. jamie bell is lying on
his belly talking to me about
my poems. he likes my poems.
i'm surprised to learn that
he has been aware of
me, and my poems, and has
been reading my poems, for
over the past 10 years or
so. they turn him on.
he likes them a lot. he
tells me these things. i like
his movies. they turn me on.
i like them a lot. i tell
him these things. he smiles
demurely, pushes the
covers off of himself,
and lies there with
his smooth sexy butt
exposed. he kind of
wriggles it.
i smear a little
aveeno body lotion
onto my cock.
i climb on top of
him and push my
cock between his butt
cheeks, oh so muscular,
oh so smooth. i don't

push my cock into his
anus, i just move
it back and forth
in the tight space
between his two hot
moist butt
cheeks. he seems to
enjoy this activity
quite a lot, and,
when i spurt cum
onto his back, i notice
that he's spurting cum
onto the sheet beneath him.
we get out of bed,
i wipe off his back
with a soft towel,
and then i sniff the
spot of cum he left
on the sheet. smells
warm and musky, and
really quite good.
"would you like to
take a shower with me?"
he asks.
"duh," i say.
we stand in the shower,
soaping each other up,
talking poetry, talking
movies, talking
the life of
talk, the mysteriosity
of athletics, screwed
into the milkshake that
is the state of the universe,
chocolate, and vanilla,
and, the most elusive of them
all: the smooth and

delectable,
raspberry cream.

the british are coming

calling out the guard to protect my misspent youth
is like getting a fly swatter to kill a mountain lion.
calling out a sexy naked big-dicked teenage boy
to protect my misspent old age is like
commanding everyone, everywhere, to
cease masturbating, once and for all.
people keep expecting logic and
reasonable transitions from Point A to
Point B. people have all kinds of
expectations. hopes and dreams,
vaulted hypotheses of the ease of
testing what is right and what is
wrong, and sensing the earnest value of
good movies when coupled with
too much wine. i tell you,
when that sexy naked big-dicked teenage boy
is lying on his back on top of his bed
at midnight, and his big throbbing dick
is hard as a rock, and he's trying to
follow the rules against masturbation,
and he's looking at himself
in the mirror that's mounted over his
dressertop, but which conveniently
shows his entire beautiful slim tawny naked
body within the confines of its
metallic frame, it's difficult for this
sexy naked big-dicked teenage boy
to keep his fingers off his
big throbbing dick, and
he smiles into the mirror,
as he waits for his erection
to subside, on its own, and
thereby relieve him of decisions,
and acts of retrogression, as
he slithers succinctly into
that state of mind where

peacocks stand in the treetops
and scream their heads off,
their big feathers fluffed up
and spread out, all
shiny in the noon-day sun.

golden age penis skeleton

the sexy naked big-dicked teenage boy had reached
the point in his masturbatory development where
he liked to whap his dick against his belly.
in other words, he liked to lie on his back atop
his bed,
and with the fingers of one hand hold onto
his dick so
that he could knock the top of his dick
against his belly, rhythmically, whap
whap whap.
the sexy naked big-dicked teenage boy
especially savored the feel of his
big purple dickhead as he knocked
the top of it against his smooth
tight belly. whap whap whap.
oh yes,
the sexy naked big-dicked teenage boy
loved to lie there atop his bed on his
back whapping the top of his big hard
dick against his nice smooth and tight
belly. this procedure made a definite
"whap whap whap" sound and one
night he was lying in bed masturbating
using that method and
making that "whap whap whap" sound
as the top of his big hard dick whapped
against his belly,
and his roommate said "what
are you doing?"
his roommate was also a sophomore
in college. his roommate was in
the top bunk.
he himself was in the bottom bunk.
his roommate was also a very good-looking
guy.
so, the mood he was in,

the sexy naked big-dicked teenage boy
who was currently masturbating
and making that "whap whap whap" sound
said: "i'm doing this new kind of
masturbation i've starting liking where
i whap the top of my dick against my belly.
it feels great, especially the part where my
my nice sensitive dickhead whaps against
me."
and, while saying these words to
his sexy roommate,
the sexy naked big-dicked teenage boy
is making that "whap whap whap" sound
as he continues masturbating using this
"whap whap whap" methodology.
in a couple of seconds, the sexy roommate
replies, "that's what i thought you
were doing," and then HE, the sexy roommate,
begins making that sound himself, as he
whaps the top of his own big smooth dick
against his own nice taut belly.
so both boys are lying in their bunks,
masturbating in this "whap whap whap"
method, neither boy seeing
the other, but both boys entirely aware
of what is going on, and very soon,
they are pacing themselves using
the exact same rhythm. their
"whap whap whaps" are synchronized
exactly, and then both sophomore college boys,
the sexy naked big-dicked teenage boy
and his hot sexy roommate,
are chuckling good-naturedly,
lying there masturbating rhythmically,
and the sexy naked big-dicked teenage boy
says to his roommate,
"any second i'm gonna spurt cum" and

his sexy roommate answers back "me too"
and
the "whap whap whap" continues right along,
until a moment of silence,
during which hot smelly cum is being spurted
in great big gooey gushy quantities.
then, both boys get out of bed
and start wiping the cum off
their chests and bellies with
dirty t-shirts,
and
the lights in their room are still
off
but
suddenly
the sexy naked big-dicked teenage boy
turns on the overhead light
and both boys stand there
staring at each other,
their big dicks still mostly
hard, their bodies young
and beautiful and sweaty,
they've never done anything like
this before, nothing sexual like
this, with each other, or with
any other guy for that matter,
and
they just go on staring at each
other like this is the most
amazing thing they've ever done
in their whole entire
lives
and, years later,
all graduated,
employed, with attractive
wives and smart sassy kids,
each of those two guys

occasionally thinks back
on that night in the dorm,
and then each of those
two guys grins, licks
his lips, and
smiles really really
big.

taking credit for sunday

monsters rise up out of the ocean and attack
the land. then, as if thinking they have done
something good, they wait to be patted
on the head by sexy naked big-dicked teenage boys.
then, in addition, they roll onto their sides
and offer their assholes to be fucked
by the sexy naked big-dicked teenage boys who
now have full raging hardons. what
sexy naked big-dicked teenage boy, and in
that state of arousal, could resist
that kind of offer? and so,
the sexy naked big-dicked teenage boys
pat the monsters on the head
and fuck them up the ass. then,
they roll apart, these freshly-fucked
head-patted monsters and
the sexy naked big-dicked teenage boys
who have just head-patted them and butt-fucked them,
and the monsters slink back into
the sea, once again, thinking they have done
something good. then the sexy naked big-dicked
teenage boys lie there alone on the sand,
staring up at the sky, worshipping faith and
hope, and craving the meaning of charity.
when the time arrives
for the sexy naked big-dicked teenage boys
to spurt another load of
cum, the
warning sirens go off and everyone
starts milling about. there is
high anxiety on the beach. nothing
seems certain, and it is
only the very lucky, who
bend over, wait, and
grab ahold of
their own ankles, as

the sexy naked big-dicked teenage boys
roam about, making difficult,
though well-reasoned, choices.

kangaroo vine gold rush

ralph the nation and pantomime the stars,
the manikins are coming to town. and why is
it, you may ask, that manikins have no
genitalia? males or females, the
manikins just don't have these organs.
the sexy big-dicked teenage boys are standing
in front of a window display, where
all the manikins are still nude, and
are just this moment being dressed, and
it is hard not to notice that
none of these manikins have
genitalia. "where are the guys' dicks?" says
one of the sexy big-dicked teenage boys.
"and where are the girls' cunts?" says
another of the sexy big-dicked teenage boys.
then, the sexy big-dicked teenage boys
stand there a while longer, until
the manikins are mostly dressed,
and then,
nearing sunset,
the sexy big-dicked teenage boys
head on over to the house
where one of them lives,
and they take off all their
clothes, and they look at
each other's genitals. and by
look, i mean really look.
these sexy naked big-dicked teenage boys
examine each other's genitals,
scrutinize each other's genitals,
talk about each other's genitals,
and, the general consensus is,
that everybody here looks real good naked,
and that everybody here has real nice
genitals, and that boy manikins everywhere
should definitely have genitals, too.

by then, all the sexy naked big-dicked
teenage boys have pretty much
fallen in love with each other,
and they touch each other
in warm, friendly, and
overtly sexual ways. in fact, when
the word "orgy" is spoken,
there is instant agreement,
and
even the sexy male manikin that's
been hidden in the
mother's closet, gets to
take part. none of the
boys are surprised to see
that this particular manikin
has a penis,
or that his
eyes are startlingly
blue.

the evolutionary squawk

"ambrosia for the masses,
but only turnips for the elite?"
thinks the sexy naked big-dicked teenage boy.
"that doesn't seem fair, now does it?"
**

the sexy naked big-dicked teenage boy
is bothered by a sense
of fairness, by a sense of what
is, and is not, fair play in
the day-to-day operations of the world.
**

"and why should the masses
be the main market for
all the big beautiful blockbuster movies, and,
for us, the elite, there's just
these scrawny little indie films?"
**

oh yes, the sexy naked big-dicked teenage boy
knows quite well that his own
status is firmly with the elite,
and that he, and the masses,
have never traveled the same path.
**

the sexy naked big-dicked teenage boy
is a worrier, too, as he
stands there in
a secluded spot in the forest,
staring up into the sky, as
if searching for answers.
**

the sexy naked big-dicked teenage boy
is tugging on his own big
sweet beautiful dick,
now hard as a rock,
as the birds sing, and the
butterflies flutter about.

there's a droplet of perfectly
clear, and sticky, pre-cum at
the tip of his dick, and
he's just about at the moment
of orgasm.
**

"this business of equality,"
thinks the sexy naked big-dicked teenage boy,
as he tugs on his own big
beautiful dick, "when
clearly i'm good-looking and gifted
and sexy as hell, is certainly
a matter for further contemplation,"
thinks the sexy naked big-dicked teenage boy,
as the moment of orgasm
arrives, his cum begins to
spurt, and his tight little
nipples tingle like bright
copper pennies, hitting the
pavement, as the traffic
slows to a stop.

5 lizards

i mean, really, the world didn't
end yesterday; what are the
chances it's going to end today?
**

while the two sexy naked big-dicked
teenage boys are down by
the creek, in the most secluded part
of the forest,
tugging gently on each other's
big hard smooth dicks
and watching each other
spurt cum,
they both feel sizzly sexy
orgasmo hot, and they
love watching each other spurt
cum, love the feel of each
other's big hot smooth thick
dicks throbbing between
their eager grasping fingers.
finally, though, they get
dressed, and go on
home to their separate
houses, and to the
loneliness that they find there.
**

when the planet saturn
glows in the sky,
most people can't
recognize saturn
from any other dot of
light in the nighttime sky.
that's perfectly understandable
everyone can't be an astronomer.
just think of the
cost.

streetcar

when splashing around in the bath water,
the sexy naked big-dicked teenage boy likes
to see his dickhead sticking up out of the
water, and feel the contrast of the coolish
air on his dickhead, and the hot water
on the rest of his dick, and on his
balls, and on all the rest of
him that is submerged beneath the
water.
generally the sexy naked big-dicked teenage boy
likes to take a shower instead of a bath,
but, sometimes, he's in the mood
for a bath,
sprawling out in the tub
full of hot water,
looking at his dickhead sticking
up out of the water, watching
his dick get hard, and then harder,
and then rock hard throbbing eager
to spurt cum,
and the skin of
his balls contract, and
feeling the sensation of
his balls held tight in
their sac,
tight against that spot
right between his legs,
but slightly forward
of that spot,
and
lying in the tub,
he kind of lifts
his pelvis,
and thrusts his entire
big hot wet cock
and

his wet shiny scrotum
out of the water
and
his pubic hair
wet and curly
and waterbound against
his skin
and it is then
that, without even touching his dick,
the sexy naked big-dicked teenage boy
spurts a big load of cum
and watches it hit his
chest and belly
and sometimes (and this is not just
showing off) the wall behind
his head
and
then
the sexy naked big-dicked teenage boy
settles back down into the tub,
the hot water settling over
him,
his cum kinda sliding loose
and drifting from his skin
some of it toward the surface
of the bath water,
some of it kinda
slithering bloblike
onto the bottom of
the tub
and the cum
on the wall just kinda
stuck there, suspended,
hanging on,
as if
it just plans to stay
there
forever.

flint

the sexy naked big-dicked teenage boy is
a white boy, but he wants to be a native american boy,
hopefully a native american boy from ancient times,
because he thought it would be fun to run around
mostly naked and hunt animals and fuck like a savage.
the sexy naked big-dicked teenage boy
didn't know much at all about how native americans
really lived, but in his head he
has this image of himself,
this image of
himself wearing almost nothing at all
and he is carrying
a bow and arrow, or a spear,
running down a big savage beast of some kind
with a group of his sexy wild half-naked friends,
running down that beast, a big furry bison perhaps,
and stabbing it with spears and shooting it with arrows,
and then skinning it and cutting it apart
and bringing its butchered parts back
to the womenfolk in the village
and there would be a big feast
and lots of mostly-naked dancing
and then a night of wild rampant
fucking of the womenfolk
and lots of spurting of cum
and many many orgasms
that night to celebrate
the killing of that big hairy bison.
meanwhile,
as
the sexy naked big-dicked teenage boy
was having these thoughts,
he is standing in the middle
of the forest all alone
tugging on his big thick hard
sturdy dick, and he is about

to spurt cum
and his tiny little nipples
are tingling
and the tips of the pubic hairs
on his scrotum
are moving lightly in the warm summer breeze
and their hairy movements is causing
his scrotum to tingle with
unbelievably strong readiness
to urge his big throbbing dick right along
in spurting out a big
gooey series of blobs of
hot runny musky-scented cum
and as the sexy naked big-dicked teenage boy
tugs on his dick
and awaits the actual moment
of spurting cum
he watches a little flock of birdies,
chickadees they are,
and he wonders
how anyone
could ever
kill
an animal,
could ever kill
any animal,
all those sweet animals
in the world,
birds and beasts and giant whales in the sea
but
when the orgasm does begin and he is now spurting
his cum
and his cum is jetting out of him
in big gooey jolts of orgasmo-heat
he is a wild native american mostly-naked
boy
running down a bison

and stabbing
it
right through the
eye, his half-naked boyfriends
shouting like
savages,
their dicks
flopping up down back
and forth, under
very little
cover.

clorox bleach

the twin boys had been having sex with each other
longer than they could remember.
perhaps they'd first sucked each other's dicks
inside their mother's womb.
they'd grown up sexy slender and gorgeous, and
all through high school they'd
done it: had secret sex with each other.
and, all through college,
it had been easy since they
were roommates in the dorm, and
then, in their own apartment.
they'd never "cheated" on each other,
never had sex with anyone else.
sometimes, after a particularly
tough academic week in college,
exam week for example,
well, the weekend following
that, they spent that entire
weekend in bed, "recuperating
thru recreation," having every
kind of sex with each other
that they'd ever had, and adding
in a couple more variations, as well,
"for extra fun."
**

then,
after college, they got
jobs in the same city,
and lived together,
and continued having sex
with each other all the time,
until, one day, seemingly
out of the blue,
one of the twins
said it should stop.
it was "just wrong."

they had a brief discussion,
and,
it was decided that they
would continue living together,
but would no longer have
sex with each other.
**

their world turned dark
and stormy. alone in
their now-separate beds, they cried
themselves to sleep nearly
every night.
**

finally, the twin who
had initiated the "no-sex" rule
moved out,
and left his twin brother all
alone.
**

as the century ended, and
trees everywhere began dying
of intense and
vicious insect infestations,
the sexy twin boys
continued their lives alone,
full of shame,
confused about the
guilt, lonely for
each other's arms, dicks,
asses,
the taste of each other's cum.
**

finally,
when they both thought everything
looked pretty much hopeless,
one weekend
they had a major "slip-up"

in the shower of their suite in
a major hotel. after, their
eyes shining like
four super-nova stars,
they said
to each other, and quietly, too,
just to heck with everything,
and moved back in together,
and
quietly lived,
life.

xo

when my college roommate and i were both college juniors,
we were taking a nap, him in his bed, and, a few
feet away, me in my bed. he woke me up
saying "damn damn damn" as he jumped up out
of his bed and
rushed over to his closet.
"what?" i said. "what!?"
he didn't tell me what was going on for a moment,
but, as he was taking off his pants and underpants,
he said, "a wet dream in a NAP," he said. "who
has a wet dream while taking a NAP?!"
"um," i said, trying to be friendly,
non-judgemental, kind, "i guess
it can just happen."
"guess so," he said, as he pulled
on a fresh pair of underpants, and
a new pair of pants. "on top
of that, i'm late for class," he
said, rushing out the door
of our little one-room
efficiency apartment.
leaving me there, alone.
still lying in my bed.
i got out of bed.
i went to his closet.
his pants, and his underpants,
the ones he'd been wearing
during the nap, were
still warm, and still had fresh
cum on them. the smell
was magic. cum. heavy,
musky. his cum.
my hot sexy roommate's
cum. my own dick was
hard as a rock.
i held his pants

and underpants
under my nose,
and i jerked off
into my own underpants.
bam! happened fast. i came.
just. like. that.
then. i felt a little
sick, almost nauseated.
i was in love with my
roommate. he was
sexy, sweet, and
a straight boy.
i was secretly,
not even sure yet
that it was so, but
pretty sure.
i was gay.
and in love
with him. and
had just jerked off
with his warm cum
in front of my face.
alone in our apartment.
my own underpants sticky
with my own hot cum.
i looked in the big
mirror on the back
of the bathroom door.
i was sexy, too. i was
good-looking, too.
would that ever
matter to him? what
would i do if it
did?
no, him a straight
boy, and me,
secretly gay. the

odor of hot
cum in that
little room,
the taste of
hunger, the swirling
whirlwind
of ache.

votive wintertime offering

the sylvan strains of syracuse
disrupt the football players in
their locker room.
the tumescence of the situation
is sex toy phallus, balls furry hairy
brush-like trimmed and all stages in
between. stag-night the suppository
delight of beer-tube enemas.
gruff voices of aftershave
enoble the basest aspirations.
the stitching on the footballs
frankensteinian in flexibility.
only the choicest sirloin,
the potatoes french or mashed,
nothing else seems to satisfy
the constant want need eat it
gotta have it down the throat
tube to belly direct flight
if at all possible. tongue
might be tickled, but just
get the good stuff to the gut.
there are legendary quagmires
in the way the sexy naked
men line up along the
showerroom walls, the hot
steaminess pile-driving over
the surfaces of their
anatomical extravagances,
even the wet shiny lip
twists, the chins wiped
with the lotion of
pure ticklish notions
greta the garbo,
stan the man.

blips

the sexy naked big-dicked teenage boy is
sitting in his bedroom, on the edge
of his bed, his feet on the floor,
saying, kind of quietly, kind of
whispered, but kind of right outloud,
"sorry for the apple pie.
sorry for the cream puffs. sorry for
the cum stain on the rug. sorry for
the beer. sorry for the wine.
sorry for the whiskey."
the sexy naked big-dicked teenage boy
has a full thick raging hardon,
and he is gently tugging on his
big thick dick, as he says,
"sorry for the toothbrush. sorry
for the amaretto cupcakes. sorry for
the D on the biology test. sorry
for the time i came in michael's
hair." the sexy naked big-dicked teenage boy
wriggles his toes into the fibers of his
nice thick rug, and he tugs on
his big hard dick some more,
and he says, "sorry for
the airplanes. sorry for
the war machines. sorry
for the dissolution of
hopes, dreams, and aspirations
of greatness."
the sexy naked big-dicked teenage boy
is tugging faster, he knows
he's about to cum, knows he's
about to go into electro-convulsive
spikes of shock as his cum goes
spurting out the peehole of
his big thick purple dickhead.
"sorry for the pentagrams on

the livingroom wall. sorry for
the watercress sandwiches. sorry for
the lion languishing in the
city zoo. sorry for the
pace of traffic, the sincerity
of useless desire." and at
this moment,
the sexy naked big-dicked teenage boy
starts spurting cum, and
it goes all over his sexy smooth
chest and flat taut belly
and dribbles into his
pubic hair and he stares
up at the ceiling and
pants and gasps with
the sheer electro-joy-jolt
of his extremely excellent
high-voltage orgasm and
then he says,
"sorry for the
pumpkin pie. sorry for the
turkey. sorry for the
methodology of
digestion. sorry for
the horsehair in the
dead old pillows."
then,
the sexy naked big-dicked teenage boy
stands up, wipes the cum off of himself
with an old t-shirt, tosses
the t-shirt into
the laundry basket,
and greets the rising sun
with a wink, a nod,
and a
daub of spit, aimed
accurately at

the wall behind
his bed. "bullseye,"
he says.
"sorry."

shall we first wash the sheets?

california the states
mitosis the crawl
the long lean drawl of the
gentle sexy blond farmboy
verizon the best phone
network in the world
mitochondrial ooze easily
cleaned up with just a bit of bleach
of course you know a man's
reach should exceed his grasp
that was the motto of my
high-school yearbook
i was a copy editor
i was a young naive suicidal mess.
the lost continent had
barely been found
a loss for words as
the sexy naked
big-dicked farmboy
put the tip of his
penis right in my mouth
the aroma of
puerile sex the
sparks of
daggerbreath, the
height of the
pinnacle of
pink-lippy
success.

mr. cat

the boats skittered upon the surface of the sea
like ballerinas upon a smooth slippery stage.
all the boats looked very feminine,
except for the dark one, with big sails.
that boat looked masculine, like the lone male ballet
dancer on the stage. the big dark boat slid around,
knocking into all the little boats,
making them quiver and bounce and yawl.
soon, the only boat on the smooth
glassy surface of the sea was the
dark boat. in it were
14 naked men, all of them handsome,
sexy, big-dicked, broad-shouldered,
swaggering. they seemed pretty
proud of themselves. "we sure got
us them girls, didn't we?" they
said amongst themselves. "we really
got 'em good! kah-fucking-pow!!" daylight
faded to night. the 14 big-dicked
naked men
sat on the deck, staring up
into the sky, contemplating
the stars and the moon.
they loved their lives.
they adored the smell
of the sea, the taste
of lost virginity, especially when
served upon a tray
of dripping wet kelp, strands
of algae still attached,
pubic and
mild-mannered, like superman,
before he met lois. when the
wind picked up,
the sails made a lot of noise,
and then settled down to

a nice steady bulge,
even-tempered, perhaps even
sane.

dragon's tooth

when watering the biggest flowers in the flower bed,
he tried not to show favoritism,
but he was a sexy big-dicked young man, and
found himself naturally gravitating toward bigger
things. still, though, the sexy big-dicked young man
cherished the small, weak, and frail, and
never gave the littlest flowers sub-standard rations.
it was just that the biggest flowers needed, well,
they needed more.
more water. more fertilizer. it was just the
way the world worked.
the sexy big-dicked young man understood that,
and tried not to question.
so, he went about his chores being kind
and gentle, but, not unrealistic about
the ways of the world. the biggest flowers
got the most water, because they really needed it.
the petite flowers got less water, because, well,
they didn't need as much water, and, in fact,
would suffer from ill effects if too much
water were given to them.
**

the sexy big-dicked young man really
did have what an average person would
call a tremendous dick. huge.
length, thickness, big-thick purple head, too.
to use an old-fashioned phrase,
the sexy big-dicked young man was just
"hung like a goddamn fucking horse."
and he was so good-natured, too.
warm, and gentle, and friendly.
**

one day while watering the flowers,
the sexy big-dicked young man was
feeling especially sexual and so he took
off all his clothes and watered

the flowers in the nude.
his dick was hard and throbbing,
and, as he wrapped the fingers of
one hand around the nozzle, he
wrapped the fingers of his
other hand around the shaft
of his big thick throbbing dick.
mostly all the way around the
shaft, that is, not that
they would reach all the
way around. anyhow, he
watered the flowers and
jerked on his dick,
and watered some more
flowers, and jerked on
his dick some more,
and, when the moment
of orgasm occurred, as
it always did in such
circumstances, he
spurted all his cum
onto the littlest flowers.
drenched them. smeared
them in slime. then, he
waited, his dick still
hard and dripping cum,
the nozzle directed
at all the flowers
except for the ones so recently
drench-smeared in his cum.
he began to hear sucking
sounds. the littlest flowers
were twitching and writhing
and making little sounds, little
sucking sounds. soon,
in a matter of moments, actually,
they were just as big as

the biggest flowers in
the garden.
the sexy big-dicked young man
was astonished, happy,
and went quite wild.
still naked, he danced around
like a savage, yelping and
praying to pagan gods
and goddesses whose
names he suddenly found
that he knew.
**

the littlest flowers were
now gigantic, big as
sunflowers.
the sexy naked big-dicked young man
bent down and knealt before
them, as if in worship,
as if in the purest throes
of the purest religio-sacrosanct
ecstasy.
**

he sighed deep, breathed
in the mucosal scent of
the whole entire world, which had suddenly
become this one great big under-glass
hot-house bridal bouquet jolly green
giant of a room—
**

when last seen,
the sexy big-dicked young man
was still naked, running through
the greenhouse, until
he seeped through the glass,
evaporated into
plumes of the
purest whitest silk.

radar detected
unusual wave patterns
in the fibre of
milwaukee, and
palm trees in florida
grew coconuts the
size of
volkswagens— not
their cute little bugs, but
those great big
gaudy sex-flavor-tone
busses.

twice that many

speaking of possibilities,
it was the POSSIBILITY of possibilities
that excited him,
that made him sweat.
as he stood naked and alone
in the forest, naked and ultra-sexy,
the slinky sinewy big-dicked boy
thought of POSSIBILITIES:
the trees suddenly
bursting into flames,
the sky turning beet-red,
the salamanders transforming
themselves into scale-covered balloons,
rising up into the rapidly-melting bubble-gum
wrappers that had once been clouds.
ah yes,
the naked slinky sinewy big-dicked boy
saw the
fall of long-lasting civilizations,
the
treaclization of dietary programs,
the
missions of long-lost fighter-pilots completed
afterall.
ah, the POSSIBILITY of possibilities.
endless and eternally mutable.
the naked slinky sinewy big-dicked boy
watched
as the protozoa evolved into
big-boned vapid-eyed dinosaurs,
the ocean's kelp
wrapping itself around
sexy mermen who fucked
ever-willing dolphins who then
gave birth to extra-terrestrial
vats of soft bubbly panna cotta.

ah,
yes,
the naked slinky sinewy big-dicked boy
dreamed and believed and yearned
and hungered
as he tugged on his own big
thick nice long hard-as-a-rock dick,
and spurted cum
into the temporality of time and
reason,
flights to the
watershed regions of
cowboy wranglers and
monetary
manipulations
a solitary tri-folded sheet of white shiny paper
artfully mounted on a big
lonely
museum wall, the marble
floors of the restrooms there
so very peaceful,
so angry,
so detailed in their splashes
of sticky little drops of
barely yellow piss.

secure scaffolding

the fragility of the species,
bones piled on bones,
the depth indeterminate,
but surely must be several
hundred feet. a
bulldozer wouldn't be
the choice of those
who manage quality
museums of antiquity,
but, bulldozers
do get the job done,
revealing enough
for all the
plunderers, and
their kin, too.
**

centuries later,
alone in his little
office, just his third
day on the job, the
fresh college graduate
blonde blue-eyed good-looking
big-dicked boy
sits with his door
locked and looks
at porn on his
computer screen
and he frees his
big dick and spurts
a load of cum
into a handful
of kleenexes.
after that, he
feels much better,
but a bit lucky
that no one knocked

on his door, no one wanted
anything, no one
tried to get in
while he was
tugging on his big
dick and spurting
a load of cum and then
re-adjusting himself,
his clothing.
his nice tight fashionable
trousers.
**

after work,
the fresh college graduate
blonde blue-eyed good-looking
big-dicked boy
stops by the bone-pit on
his way back to his
cute little apartment,
looks at the top level
that has recently been exposed,
frightening creatures,
those massive skulls,
those deep evil-looking
eye sockets. he grabs
a loose skull and
takes it with
him, puts it on
the coffee table
in his living room,
dances naked around
it, welcomes it
home.

suspenders

when packing up a suitcase,
there may be a moment of profuse profanity,
gnashing teeth, and grave indecision.
at least,
that's the way it was for
the sexy big-dicked teenage boy,
a college freshman,
going off to visit his boyfriend.
what was he going to be doing
with his boyfriend, other than
having sex with him, that is?
where were they going to go?
what kinds of clothes should
he bring? and should he choose
the standard toiletries, or something
extra? a new flavor of toothpaste,
perhaps? an extra-zingy one?
the sexy big-dicked teenage boy
stood beside his bed, his suitcase
on top of it,
and looked at the contents:
shirts, underpants, socks,
pants, t-shirts,
this, that, the other. then
the sexy big-dicked teenage boy
actually whimpered.
how could he be expected to make
these kinds of decisions?
decisions about packing a suitcase.
decisions about ANYTHING?
the sexy big-dicked teenage boy
sat down on the chair beside
his bed.
he stared at his suitcase.
his boyfriend was sure
hot, and a nice guy, too.
it would be good to see him.

good to have sex with him. REAL good.
once he was there.
but, this, the preparation,
the packing of the suitcase, the
deciding and indeciding
and re-deciding,
was just obnoxious.
suddenly,
the sexy big-dicked teenage boy stood up,
left everything where
it was, on the bed,
and went out to his
car, and started driving.
no suitcase! no toiletries!
those kinds of decisions, no longer
necessary! he breathed in the
fresh air, and sighed a real big sigh.
he was driving pretty darn fast, and,
every now and then, in a final act
of decision, he took off an
article of clothing, and tossed it
out the window.
**

by the time he got there,
the utter foolishness of
love— young & stark & ultra dick-friendly—
just made it all,
even more friendly,
home of the land-scrubbers,
greasy on the tip
of that golly dang
slick and slippery tweak on
the nipples, the
taste of silence, the
shy shimmy thrust of that quick,
gooey,
slime-drippy
spoon.

social protocol

the shrimp popper button having been pushed,
and then played in triumph,
the happy little group ate their
shrimp perfection meal and
washed it down with tasty gossip.
and a bit of bubbly, too.
then, the night nearly done,
each and every one went home,
and settled into bed,
burping shrimp vapors into
the warm night air,
the sky a virtual parakeet
of stars.

spitfire

i have smiled politely at crap that was supposed
to be funny, but wasn't.
i have said that i like the taste of certain
foods that were served to me when i didn't like
the stuff at all.
i have swum in cold water that was so cold
it hurt, and then described my swim as "invigorating."
i have replied politely to people who
have said dumb, and i mean really dumb,
absolutely cretinously asinine, stuff to me.
i have compromised, and settled, and appeared
to have been "placated," and "soothed."
yet,
in reality,
i'm angry nearly all the time.
"FUCK YOU" is always ready
on my tongue, but
hiding out,
just beneath
the tip.

some more moss on that memory sandwich

at the filling station, the wayward bus docks,
and spills its water.
7 sexy adolescent boys
get up, go get something to drink,
piss, get a snack, and talk
to each other about things
of itinerant nature.
then, back on the bus,
the 7 boys, all chosen as their
high school's representatives to
this year's American Legion Boys State,
chat, and doze, and find hope in the
certainty that Williamsburg, Va,
is a nice town, with a good
campus (William & Mary), and
that, with a little luck and
good campaigning, charisma,
and charm, each of them
will be mock-elected to mock-office
and pass mock-bills and enact
mock-legislation in
the mock-assembly for the common good
of all those mock-assembled.
The American Legion wants
dreamers and doers. these 7
boys selected from their high school's
best and brightest
are there to do a job, make
their high school proud,
and indicate their
bulwark of society to
the culture of
belief systems that
are good, noble, and true.
hot dogs for dinner,
and

at night,
sleeping two to a dorm
room
on a campus lent to them
for the duration of their
stay (4 days),
there are
a plethora of
fuzzy-headed dreams,
some of them focused like
needle points going for the
hole of the button, some
of them drifting
like
american marigolds, just
before the
harvest.
**

i was one of the American
Legion Boys State boys in
that group of 7.
many years ago.
while on that bus heading
to that year's
American Legion Boys State, a classmate
of mine, Greg, who was tall
dark and handsome,
put his head on my shoulder
and slept while he thought that
i, too, was asleep.
all these years later
(i'm 59 years
old now), i still remember
that moment: Greg's head
resting on my shoulder,
my heart pounding, my heart
is pounding so hard i'm

afraid he'll hear it and wake
up and confirm what i'm thinking.
what i'm thinking is i love
this moment and i love
that Greg is resting his
head on my shoulder
and i love Greg and
i love Greg
and
i love Greg and
the word
"homosexual"
flashes like neon
on my forehead,
Greg's head
resting on my
shoulder,
please don't let him hear
my faggot heartbeat
don't let anyone see that
neon light stuck to
my forehead or
hear that bass-drum heart thump
as the bus nears its
destination,
as i see the King's Palace,
Williamsburg awaits.
**

now,
years later: things that i know:
i know that i'm a homosexual,
i know that Greg isn't, that he
never was, that
he got married to his high-school
sweetheart. i knew he wasn't
a homosexual when he put
his head on my shoulder on

that bus trip. i knew his was
an innocent, friendly, non-sexual,
guy-on-guy gesture, that he
was sleepy, wanted a comfortable place
to rest his head. a basketball
player, he'd no doubt done
this, slept on
their sleeping shoulders, with other
sleeping straight
guys on other bus trips, basketball
trips, teammates, buds.
**

but the sweetness of the gesture,
his head resting on my shoulder,
him asleep,
on me, me just a regular guy
at that moment, this,
just one of the things
regular guys do with regular guys,
affirming my normality
the most normal guy
on the bus sleeping
on me
my heart pounding and pounding,
me pretending to sleep,
wondering why he didn't
wake up to the
pounding of my heart.
the sweetness of the gesture.
the normalness
of normality.
**

Williamsburg awaits.
me getting off the bus,
going to my room assignment,
no memory of who i was
assigned to.
somebody who wanted to

get elected to something.
somebody, now that i
think back, somebody who did get
elected to something.
Williamsburg was
Williamsburg was
no fun
at all.

butter or margarine

in the squiggle brigade of death-centric studies,
the urgency of flippancy cannot be dismissed.
the detritus of destruction is
not to be confused with the pleasure of procreation.
nothing is to be confused with anything,
even though everything is clearly confusing.
all one has to do is admit the truth
of the error. it's not that difficult,
when faced with all kinds of irrefutable evidence
to the correctness of judgement, whether
impaired, or not.
one sloshes around and does the
best one can, or not, depending
on various attitudinal and environmental
factors.
for a sexy naked big-dicked young man,
the urgency of orgasm,
the need to share his big hard
thick dick with an appreciative audience,
can be quite the motivator.
a sexy naked big-dicked young man
loves to spurt cum, loves
the near-vicious electro-jolt of
orgasm, and,
sometimes,
sharing the experience with
another sexy naked big-dicked young man
makes the experience even hotter,
sexier, and more vibrant. also,
there's the question of loneliness,
which has never been satisfactorily
resolved. is the best orgasm
to be had when one is alone,
or when one is in the company of company?
these are difficult
questionalities, the

uncertainty and muddiness
of perfect black-n-white answers,
a constant befuddlement,
a red poppy on a plain
of green foliage,
the click of the crickets
at midnight,
the sky a perfect wash
of yellow-green stars.

climate

you know, being an
alcoholic manic depressive homosexual
is never easy,
but one copes.
some days are easier than others.
i lucked out when the guy i fell
in love with, fell in love with me, too.
that helped a lot.
i don't know which i've been the longest:
probably i'd have to say i've been
manic depressive the longest.
after that, i figured out i was homosexual.
after that, i became an alcoholic.
there were some years in between,
a few jigs and jags,
but that's kind of the jist of things.
i'm 59 years old now.
i still remember being
a skinny sexy blond teenage boy,
naked in a secluded spot in the woods,
the sunlight on my hot young body,
my dick hard and thick
and i'm tugging on it
my pubic hair a curly frenzied restless nest
and i'm awaiting the absolute manic ecstasy
of a joyous orgasm, good and gushy
splats of cum, splatting onto
the crackly dry leaves,
there in the summer sunshine.
there've always been good times.
amongst the bad.
being an
alcoholic manic depressive homosexual
has worked out okay for me, i guess.
i sometimes think about other
ways of being in the world,

things i might have changed,
things i might still change,
but,
i'm married to a good man,
i drink what i want,
my moods don't tyrannize me
as much as they once
did,
and,
well,
after 59 years,
you sorta get used to stuff.

no excuses

i'm 58 years old now, and
i remember the days when i was
in college and lived in the dorm
and the main criteria for a friend
seemed to be he was sexy and he
made me laugh. and we
talked all the time. about
everything. some nights,
standing there in the big
dorm showerroom on my hall,
talking naked to each other,
about anything, everything,
grades, mold, food, eyes move
up and down each other's
bodies, nothing
sexual going on, and yet,
everything sexual
going on.

taste

the football players are built like refrigerators.
except for the quarterback.
the quarterback is built like a textbook anatomical drawing
of the ideal husband and perfect god-like guy. everything
is in just-right proportion. chest, hands, lips,
trachea branching into two perfectly symmetrical bronchi,
scrotum perfectly bi-lobed, testes nestling within, just
behind the relaxed fit of the quintessentially exquisite dick.
the quarterback stands there half-naked among
the refrigerators,
and he looks so out of place in his utter perfection
that it's difficult not to
wonder if the others think of him as not
really one of them, as a representative of
another species perhaps, and if
they picture a quick sudden
whirlwind carrying him away,
touseling his hair,
roughing up his balls, chafing the pink tight skin of
his lightly furred and inner thighs.
nobody says anything, but when
the quarterback strips down for his shower,
the refrigerators
crank out the ice cubes,
and then watch them melt.

surgeon general notwithstanding

although i never smoked, i used to enjoy kissing
the mouths of men who did. i liked the
taste of their lips, the tobacco-ey sultriness
of the saliva on their tongues.
their mouths tasted sexy and sensuous.
yes, i enjoyed kissing the mouths of
men who were smokers. cigarettes,
to be specific. i don't think i
ever kissed men who smoked
pipes or cigars. it seems i'd
remember a taste like that if
i'd kissed any of them. but
i do remember the taste of the
mouths of men who smoked cigarettes.
and i liked it.
and one of my favorite wetdreams
was mr.marlboro man, where has
he gone? after all these years,
and what has he got to show for
himself? i hope he's happy,
all leather and horse and smoke.

club soda

"i'll bet mack the knife ate pizza for breakfast,"
says the sweet sexy big-dicked teenage boy to his
hot sexy boyfriend, who was named rauser.
"heck, who knows what the HECK mack the knife ate
for breakfast?" says rauser.
"and who the hell WAS mack the knife?" adds rauser,
"and, furthermore," says
rauser, "just who the hell KNOWS who mack the knife was?"
"we could google that, i'll bet," says
the sweet sexy big-dicked teenage boy to rauser.
"or we could just take off the rest of our clothes
and i could fuck your sweet little ass," says rauser.
they quickly agree on the latter choice, and
while
the sweet sexy big-dicked teenage boy is
getting fucked in the ass by his hot sexy boyfriend rauser,
mack the knife materializes in their bedroom
and takes photographs.
**

turns out he's mack the photographer now.
tries to forget his past.
everyone does.

don't butter your bread on both sides

the quails in the hollow of my armpits
have taken flight,
their little beaks sharp and squawky,
their little claws scratching at the empty air,
their slight delicate feathers wispy, waifish.
a breeze has been created
by all those shrill little
flapping wings. now, all are gone: birds,
feathers, everything—
seemingly signifying, i fear, my total abandonment of the
solid agrarian principles of my ancestors,
principles on which this country was based.
**

my armpits, however, feel liberated,
free of all those feathers and beaks and claws,
and, alas, just a tad bit, lonely, too.
one grows accustomed
to a certain amount of this sort of thing, i think.
after a while, it almost
seems normal.

shortlist

green grow the peas in the heart of the winter.
it's a miracle.
but peas know what they know.
they know it's time to thrive, and bloom,
and make baby peas inside those nice sleek pea pods.
even when there are tufts of snow on the ground.
white, and crisp, nearly the essence of purity.
**

the crowd at the museum was good that
day.
everybody likes to see good paintings
of naked people.
**

the sexy naked athletic big-dicked teenage boy
was up in his room, admiring himself in
the mirror. as usual, he was so pleased with what
he saw that he started tugging on his big
hard dick until he spurted cum.
the cum splatted onto the rug, and
then soaked in. he acted like he
didn't care, because he didn't.
**

when the robin began to sing,
the certainty of the vernal arrival schedule
seemed assured,
and, by that time,
the pea vines were already
dead.
**

the rug in
the bedroom of
the sexy naked athletic big-dicked teenage boy
was kind of crispy from all the dried cum, but,
damn, if the sexy naked athletic big-dicked teenage boy
didn't look good.
**

real good.
**

and, by that, we mean,
excellent.

aqua transmissions at the twilite terrace

the door to the waterfall fell open,
and 18 beautiful big-dicked naked teenage boys
fell out. they had been a little cramped
in there, and were glad for a little
breathing room. "whew," said
one of 18 beautiful big-dicked naked teenage boys,
"lawsy!" all of the other
18 beautiful big-dicked naked teenage boys
readily agreed, nodding along,
scratching their balls, jiggling their dicks, and
so forth assenting their reliable congruence
in this sort of sentiment. they all
stood around and ate sandwiches
and drank beer, wine, vodka tonics,
and other assorted beverages.
then, the 18 beautiful big-dicked naked teenage boys
went back through the door to the waterfall,
closed the door,
and resumed life in the
splash zone, the minnows nibbling gently
at their sexy pink toes,
the crayfish so big they
were easily mistaken for lobsters.
"whew," said
one of 18 beautiful big-dicked naked teenage boys,
"lawsy!"

truce

at the sudden outbreak of fixation,
the hot gorgeous sexy big-dicked young man
fell for the tall slinky sloe-eyed teenage boy
with a clank, and a rattle, and a twank to the
knockers. kaboom the heart-thud sound.
thwack and mysterion phases of the
thigh stem package, a tweak to
the eyeballs, and a ratiocination
of the brainstem extravagances.
oh heck yeah,
the hot gorgeous sexy big-dicked young man
fell hard for the tall slinky sloe-eyed teenage boy,
and there was just no keeping the two of them
apart. in their sex bed, they
yeed and yawed and hummed and
pushed and prodded and yipped
and yammered. whimpers of
joy and explications of pleasure.
a slimy mess of semen, the spots
on the pillow inhaled as
though religious.
after their first few weeks together,
the hot gorgeous sexy big-dicked young man
and the tall slinky sloe-eyed teenage boy
showed no signs of slowing down.
a whirlwind over their heads.
eye shadow a phenomenon of
tufted titmice, screeching peacefully
amongst the sharp points of
the leaves of the holly,
red berries edible,
but only when perfectly
ripe.

the age of reason

gretchen the housebuilder hired
a sexy big-dicked teenage boy,
and, one day, after work,
gretchen asked that
sexy big-dicked teenage boy
to fuck her,
and he said all right,
and
turns out he was
the best fuck of
gretchen's big entire life.
so, they went at it
day after day,
after work,
gretchen and
that sexy big-dicked teenage boy,
up in gretchen's bedroom,
in her really nice
house that she'd built
herself,
a few years ago,
when money was easy,
and life was flush.
**

gretchen the housebuilder
and the sexy big-dicked teenage boy
spent very little time together
when they weren't fucking.
and that seemed fine to
the both of them.
but then, one day,
kind of all of a sudden,
gretchen the housebuilder
realized that she
was in love
with the sexy big-dicked teenage boy,
and she asked him to move

in with her,
and he said
no. she asked
him why not, and
he said
he was kind
of tired of her,
didn't really like her body,
felt intimidated by her,
was actually thinking
about changing jobs anyway,
just wanted out,
so long,
good-bye,
see ya 'round.
**

and that was
pretty much it.
gretchen hired another
sexy big-dicked teenage boy.
things worked out pretty well
between them.
they're still together,
as a matter of fact.
**

the first sexy big-dicked teenage boy,
the one who didn't want to move in
with her,
the one who found another job,
well,
he
eats a lot of garlic these days,
and
grew a wispy blond beard.
trying to have a conversation
with him
is like
making love

to your favorite pillow,
the one you used to fuck,
back when you were very very
young.

modern prehistory

and the egregious nature of the potsdam situation
meant that all the sexy naked big-dicked teenage boys
dreamed of toast, and jam, and a big dose of vodka-peach-sherry
as they lay on their backs alone in their skinny little
beds and spurted geysers of cum throughout the lonely
summer nights, their rooms the odor of musk, and
male, and lightly furred ballsacs, shiny with sweat.
**

one sexy naked big-dicked teenage boy in particular, named ralph,
got up out of his little bed and stood staring into the
hot night-time sky, studying the dots that were the
stars, the wisps of clouds that drifted harmlessly
between him, and them. ralph was sure that he
could see the individual little droplets of water
that composed each and every cloud, and, as
those wispy clouds drifted between him
and the stars, ralph thought that it would
be nice to fuck each and every one of
those little droplets of water, for they
seemed so all alone, even though surrounded
by others just like themselves.
**

several years later, swimming
naked in a nearby river, ralph was
now a sexy young man, in love with
all forms of water, which he drank
and bathed in, and drizzled through
his hair, the hair on top of his handsome
head, the hair that grew on his
ballsac and around his great big dick,
and that which grew on his legs, and arms,
and in the muskiness of his armpits.
swimming in that river, ralph
felt all the hairs on his body
flex and move with the current
of the river, and, once again,

ralph was insanely happy, almost
a droplet of water himself, yes, he
felt that wintergreen good.
**

when ralph fucked his wife that night,
there was a thunderstorm, and
he spurted so much cum,
it leaked out of her,
and made their bed smell
summer heat, clouds in the sky,
washing them seemed like a shame,
but, well,
soap is soap.

the indisputable logic of the parsnips

"carrots and peas. carrots and peas.
why must there always be carrots and peas?"
says the sexy big-dicked teenage boy
to his mother.
"there aren't ALWAYS carrots and peas,"
says the mother of the sexy big-dicked teenage boy.
"we have all kinds of other vegetables, too," she says.
"i like to think we have a very well-balanced diet here.
i like to think you and i eat very well in this house."
the sexy big-dicked teenage boy shrugs, kind
of apologizes, kind of. "you're right," he
says. "i guess i'm just kind of craving
stuff besides carrots and peas tonight.
but they're very good carrots and peas,"
he quickly adds. "real good, as
a matter of fact."
the mother of the sexy big-dicked teenage boy
smiles and relaxes her shoulders.
"we'll have mashed potatoes and corn-on-the-cob
tomorrow," she says. "how's that sound?"
the sexy big-dicked teenage boy smiles,
says "that sounds GREAT," and goes
on eating. there is a kind
of gentle truce at the table,
and evening settles gently
on the suburb.
**

that night, long after his
mother is sound asleep in her room,
the sexy big-dicked teenage boy is
wide awake and
naked atop his bed. he's lying on
top of the bedspread.
all the covers are underneath him.
his tight sexy little butt is
making a dent in the mattress.

the sexy naked big-dicked teenage boy
feels like an explosion of sex.
his dick is rock hard
and he's watching it throb,
jounce up and down. there's
a little dab of pre-cum at the
tip. pre-cum is a substance
he's now very familiar with,
having seen the pee-hole
at the tip of his own big dick
ooze a drop or two of
the stuff many times now.
tonight,
the sexy naked big-dicked teenage boy
touches the droplet of pre-cum
with his fingertip, wipes
that pre-cum onto his fingertip, and
then he holds his fingertip
up to his nose. he inhales
the scent: raw, tawny, musky,
sexy. then, tonight, for
the first time ever,
he sticks out his tongue
and places the droplet of
pre-cum right on the tip
of his tongue. he pulls
his tongue into his
mouth, and explores the
taste. musky, sexy,
not too threatening.
then, at that moment,
much to his surprise,
he shoots his wad of
cum and it goes
all over his chest
and belly. golly,
that was a surprise.

he hadn't even started
jerking off yet.
well, maybe later,
when he woke up
in the middle of
the night, as usual,
he'd get a chance to
jerk off nice and slow
and leisurely.
for now, though, he
wipes himself off
with a wad of kleenexes,
crawls under the covers,
and goes to sleep.
**

the next day the
waterfalls all over the world
turn orange and green
with a huge infestation
of peas and carrots. in
fact, more peas and
carrots seem to be
going over the falls
than water itself.
**

the sexy big-dicked teenage boy
has never felt more powerful,
never felt
more of a sexual presence
in the world.
and, that night, the mashed potatoes
and corn-on-the-cob,
are the best he's
ever had.

bubbles

when my ship set sail into the wilderness
of mysterious fishes and odd critters of the saline nation,
hardly anyone would talk to me.
i was too eager. too ready to show off my
keen biological knowledge and insightful
ways of observing fascinating zoological marine phenomena.
the other summer interns, were
much more relaxed about their job.
it was, for them, just a summer job,
not the best, not the worst,
and kind of an opportunity for
them to hang out with each
other and enjoy after-hours beer
and cards and talk. i didn't
even drink back then. thought
it would be bad for me. also, i
was just kind of a naive goody-two-shoes.
i was just 19, an eager-beaver college sophomore,
deliriously happy with having a real
job in my chosen field: biology.
wow. and MARINE biology at
that. specialization!
wow! i thought this was all pretty dern great.
out on the water on a marine biology
research ship, watching
the giant net slide under the
surface of the water,
knowing it was gliding and banging along
the bottom, and watching
its contents get dumped onto
the sorting table: hundreds
of fish, sometimes thousands,
all different shapes, sizes,
and colors. and pretty soon
i knew the names of all of them,
common name, scientific name,

family, and genus, and species.
oddly enough, my growing knowledge
and quick mastery of fish identification skills
did not endear me to the other
summer interns. in their eyes,
i was even more "geeky," more
of a "hotdog," a downright
"nerd."
ah well, i was having fun
anyway,
and later, when i did get
a bit more relaxed, and
was having an actual
laid-back conversation with
the chief scientist on the
ship, a tall skinny 30ish
guy with a sexy demeanor and
sweet sad eyes,
just him and me talking,
mostly about science stuff,
measuring this, identifying
that. there was
nobody else around.
he drank beer after beer.
we talked some more, and, then,
all of a sudden,
he told me something that surprised
me, something that i've always
remembered. this is what he said.
he said, "there are really only two
things i like about being alive,"
he said, as he sucked on a
can of beer.
"just two things i like:
being drunk. and
being asleep. when i'm not
drunk, i want to be

asleep. when i'm not
asleep, i want to be
drunk.
those are really the only
two things i can stand
about being alive."
there was a moment
of awkward silence.
it was
late, nearly midnight,
the surface of the
sea slick
and cold
and
black.

perpendicular to the axis of change

"squamous epithelial cells are great fun—why, just
imagine what fun one can have with
squamous epithelial cells!"
said the first tall skinny college freshman to
his tall skinny college freshman roommate.
they were both biology majors,
and they were both learning stuff,
in their dorm room, late at night,
before a big test.
"and cellular ventriloquism!" said
the second tall skinny college freshman.
"just imagine how much fun we can have with that!!"
and, actually,
both the first tall skinny college freshman
and the second tall skinny college freshman
were totally naked now.
they had just taken a shower together
in the big showerroom at the end of
their hall to "calm down, relax,
and de-stress."   now, they
were standing in
their dorm room, looking at each
other, making funny faces as they
spoke biological and
quasi-biological giggilicious terminology.
"gee, we look pretty good naked, don't we?"
said the first tall skinny college freshman,
"i mean, for two such skinny guys, i mean."
"heck no. we're not bad are we?"
said the second tall skinny college freshman.
"not bad at all."
it has become apparent that both
their dicks are getting hard,
expanding, lifting up, jutting toward
each other, as if straining to touch,
and be touched.

in no time at all,
the first tall skinny college freshman
and
the second tall skinny college freshman
are practically wrapped around each
other, enveloping each other,
tugging on each other's big sturdy
dicks, spurting cum all over
each other's hands and bellies.
then, like a sudden thunderstorm,
it is over.
the two tall skinny college freshmen
wipe up, and then grin real big.
"back to work?" says
the first tall skinny college freshman.
"back to work," says
the second tall skinny college freshman.
but neither of them makes
a move to put on his clothes,
and the night
seems like it could
be made of cellular mitochondrial
ooze,
flavored with peacock hair,
and the
scent of
wolves, begging for
licorice.

joe, would you like to say the blessing tonight?

the sensation of euphoria spoke to
the sexy naked big-dicked teenage boy like
the lover he wished he had. the lover
would be male, a year or two older than him,
with a great body, a fantastic smile,
and a huge thick dick.
ah, how the sexy naked big-dicked teenage boy
loved the sensation of euphoria.
these days, it was most fully
experienced while
he was jerking off, lying
on his back, on a frayed old
beach towel, in a secluded and sun-dappled
spot in the middle of the woods.
the sexy naked big-dicked teenage boy lived
for these moments.
they were what kept him going.
they were his reason for being
while waiting for that lover
to appear
in his life.
now,
the sexy naked big-dicked teenage boy
lay on his back on that frayed beach
towel, his legs spread wide, his knees
lifted about a foot above the towel,
and he tugged gently on his
big thick dick
while imagining that it was his
lover who was doing the tugging.
the sensation of euphoria crept
over him, licked his teeny-tiny
nipples, tongue-tipped his
tight pink little asshole,
and spread a thin film
of warm saliva all over his

lighty-furred balls.
in a few more seconds,
the sexy naked big-dicked teenage boy
began spurting cum,
and he kept on spurting cum
and spurting cum and
spurting cum for
5 minutes solid.
yes, FIVE MINUTES SOLID.
how was such a thing possible?
normal boys spurt cum for
no longer than 10 or 20 seconds at a pop.
and that's about a dozen or so
actual spurts during those 10 or 20 seconds.
but, him,
he spurted cum non-stop,
pulse after pulse, jet after jet,
for 5 solid minutes.
how many individual cum spurts was
that? 300? 400? and that jolt
of orgasm with each hard gushy spurt.
for 5 minutes solid.
5 solid minutes of complete and total euphoria.
of pure orgasmic bliss.
the 5 minutes having now passed,
the chest and belly
and pubic hair
of the sexy naked big-dicked teenage boy
drenched in cum,
he lowered his legs,
and kind of collapsed
into the towel.
the sexy naked big-dicked teenage boy
lay there staring into the gentle blue
sky,
lay there savoring the 5 generous minutes of
pure euphoria that he had just experienced,

lay there
wanting
more. more.
more.

formal thank-you letter not necessary for this gift

all the leaves fell off,
and their branches looked like
naked reaching arms, grabbing
for the sky. the tree bark
was cold and scratchy, and
the moss that was perched upon it
was brittle and
wispy, not soft
and green, but gray,
and harsh in texture,
as well as in tone.
oh how the sexy naked big-dicked teenage boy
longed for summer,
as he stood in the forest,
in the sunniest spot he could
find, but the air was still chilly
as he stood there in
the glow of the late-autumn sun,
tugging on his big hard dick,
tugging
with less enthusiasm than
he tugged on it in the summer,
when the sweat ran down
his back and butt
and dripped off his
balls and ran down his lean
muscular legs.
now, the bare branches
above him,
and all the leaves down on the ground,
the sexy naked big-dicked teenage boy
tugged on his dick
and waited for the electro-jolt of
wet sloppy orgasm,
and,
when it hit,

he spurted about 18 cum spurts
up against the bark of a nearby
tree, and watched the blotches of
his cum drip
down the filaments of
the crispy gray moss.
then, he began to shiver,
and got dressed quickly,
the chilly breath of
insistent winter
poking around inside
his nostrils,
licking the
lust right out
of his lungs.

traces of mercury

"so i see that your are vaginally active," said the
doctor to his patient.
his patient is a sexy naked colossally big-dicked young man.
"i'm not sure what you mean," said the patient to his doctor.
"i'm just a regular guy."
"and yet, clearly you are vaginally active," said the doctor.
the doctor is a mid-40s-in-age kind of guy, kind of frumpy in
his demeanor, and yet, with a sincere sense of earnestness about him.
"i'm not sure what you're getting at,"
said the sexy naked colossally big-dicked young man.
"and i'm not sure what the term 'vaginally active' actually
means," he added.
the doctor has just withdrawn his latex-covered finger
from the anus of the patient.
"i see that you let yourself get fucked in the ass
as if you were using it as a vagina, which
of course, it is not," said the doctor, trying
to sound kind and sympathetic, but, well, not really succeeding
at all.
the doctor removes the latex glove, turning it inside out as he does
so, and deposits the glove in a covered trashcan.
"you may get dressed now," said the doctor to his patient,
the sexy naked colossally big-dicked young man. "and
be assured that the fact that you are vaginally active in no way
mis-images my perception of you as a flesh-and-blood
patient with dreams and hopes and aspirations, as
well as sexual desires, wants, and kinkinesses," said
the doctor.
the sexy naked colossally big-dicked young man
stands there staring at the doctor. "i'm just
a regular guy," he said to the doctor.
"mostly, as a matter of fact, my sex life
is solo: i jerk off a lot. and i don't
insert anything at all into my ass."
"and yet, clearly you are a vaginally active young
man," said the doctor. he wrinkles up his frumpy little

nose and stares down it at his patient.
the sexy naked colossally big-dicked young man
has yet to start getting dressed. he has
an annoyed expression on his handsome face.
"i use crisco shortening when i jerk off,"
said the patient. "i smear it
on my dick and my hands. i like the texture,
the feeling of warmth, the absence of
friction."
"the application of crisco can also of course help you
in your vaginally active methodology," said
the doctor. he blinks, as kindly as possible.
"for the last time!" said
the sexy naked colossally big-dicked young man.
"i am NOT vaginally active! and i wish you
would stop using that terminology!"
"please get dressed," said the doctor.
"and don't be distressed. becoming vaginally active
is not a severe detriment to one's happiness,
healthiness, and sexual well-being."
"mainly i watch television food shows
while i'm jerking off!" said
the sexy naked colossally big-dicked young man.
"and i've never even thought of sticking a
cucumber up my ass!"
"you're thinking about it now, aren't you?"
said the doctor.
the sexy naked colossally big-dicked young man
stands there, staring at the doctor.
the patient is clearly angry.
the patient is fuming.
"i'm just a regular guy," said
the sexy naked colossally big-dicked young man.
"i just jerk off a lot. that's pretty
much the extent of my sex life."
"and these cucumbers," said the
doctor. "would they be peeled, or not?"

"i'm JUST A REGULAR GUY," said the patient.
"JUST A REGULAR GUY!!" he said again.
"being vaginally active is nothing to
be upset about," said the doctor.
"the quality of a man's life is measured
in many, many ways. most of them non-sexual,
most of them having nothing to do with whether
or not he is vaginally active."
the sexy naked colossally big-dicked young man
is getting dressed now. very quickly.
"and when did you first become vaginally active?"
said the doctor. "when was your first
vaginally active experience?"
it was then that the
sauce in the young man's refrigerator began to curdle,
and the aroma of
finely chopped onions, wafted into his kitchen.
alone in his own house that night,
the sexy naked colossally big-dicked young man
sputtered and fumed and seriously considered
treason.

walrus blood

the weather report calls for the loss of virginity,
the administration of smelling salts,
the particularly pleasant and pleasurable
pantheon of 16 sexy naked big-dicked teenage boys
taking turns fucking each other up the ass.
and, when they suck on each other's dicks,
they only taste the tip. the whole shaft
is just too beautiful.
**

the clouds are fluffy white marvels of
sea foam, suspended in the pale blue atmosphere,
raindrops not even a possibility,
not even a thought.
**

hundreds of thousands of insects
ride the air currents high above
our heads. sometimes they fall
to earth. mostly, though, they
just seem to ride.
**

all alone in his room,
jeff the tall skinny college freshman
tugs gently on his big hard well-oiled penis,
and waits
for the circus of the stars.
when the orgasm happens,
it's practically chimpanzees,
and nearly that furry,
but without all that vocalizing.
chimp vocal sounds,
those pale yellow teeth.
not what jeff was looking forward to,
and certainly not what he expected.

i reckon so, if the good lord's willin

ah the lure of the brash big-dicked cowboy.
how he can make a gay boy's heart flutter.
how he can make a gay boy's dick hard in
an instant, spurt cum in less than a minute.
the brash big-dicked cowboy is down
by the pond, the clear-water one,
where the cows don't drink.
the brash big-dicked cowboy is washing
himself off in the cool clear water.
the brash big-dicked cowboy is naked
when the gay boy spies him,
and the gay boy's dick goes instantly hard.
the gay boy stands behind a tree
and stares at the brash naked big-dicked cowboy.
the gay boy whines softly, kinda
whimpers, as the brash naked big-dicked cowboy
goes right on washing himself.
soon, real soon,
the brash naked big-dicked cowboy notices
that he's being observed.
the brash naked big-dicked cowboy speaks:
"get right over here, you!" he
says to the gay boy.
the gay boy obeys.
the gay boy sucks off the brash naked big-dicked cowboy.
the brash naked big-dicked cowboy tries to
return the favor, but the gay boy has
already spurted his cum, and
it floats in a slimy little pool on
top of the pond.
they both stare at it, nod with understanding,
and kiss each other on the lips.
things like this happen everyday.
things like this
make the rapid-fire assault of
targeted munition sites

a pea-popping pleasure,
a wealth of historical evidence
quickly demonstrable in the
annals of mercury-powered time.
"you're a good-looking boy,"
the brash naked big-dicked cowboy says
to the sweetly sexy gay boy.
"i think we should get ourselves in that
there bunkhouse right now, and pursue this
here matter."
whimpers and screams are often the
voice of
cowpoke love.

economics for bystanders

tie-dye the corrosive elements of society.
bring them down with big hay-filled barns.
the kind of hay that's golden yellow, with
threads of silver and streaks of rubicon,
after caesar crossed that goddamn river.
social norms and balances are something
worth preserving, keeping the youth
on the right track, make-shift solutions
only viable for the friskiest and the
most beautiful.
**

while the sexy big-dicked naked young man was
getting his dick sucked by his best friend jeff,
the sky was a delicate shade of misspent cash,
the greenish tinge was so overwhelming that
surely the threat of dire complications
was right close at-hand. soooo,
the sexy big-dicked naked young man
hurried himself right along and spurted
a big wad of cum right into jeff's
slimy willing mouth. jeff whimpered
with pleasure, and jerked himself
off in a hurry, spattering the taut
smooth chest of
the sexy big-dicked naked young man
whom he had just sucked off.
then,
it really began to rain
outside, and, to everyone's
delight, it was just rain.
wet. and cool. the essence
of good luck, and good fortune.
**

old cars mostly end up
flattened and twisted hunks of metal.
every now and then, though, one ends up getting

preserved, the cream of the crop,
the eye of the beholder delighted
by vanilla color, and red upholstery.
**

meanwhile, down at the golden-glow
barn,
the sexy big-dicked naked young man
and his best friend jeff
are at it again,
hay-straw the evolution of
stallions turned to stud,
don't spill any of their
stuff on the floor, it goes
for $5000 a pop.

communications satellite

knuckles crackling and toes tingling,
the sexy naked athletic big-dicked teenage boy
lifted a big bale of hay from a stack in the barn
and tossed that bale of hay against the wall.
it hit with a thud and fell onto the floor.
"not bad," the sexy naked athletic big-dicked teenage boy
said quietly to himself, for he had been trying
to see how high on the wall he could toss the hay bale,
and, when it hit a spot 12 feet above the floor, he was glad.
the sexy naked athletic big-dicked teenage boy liked
feats of strength, and, when he did good, he
felt strong, powerful, extraordinarily male,
and sexually wonderful. a young sex machine,
just zoomed up and primed right to fuck
just about anything he wanted to.
the sexy naked athletic big-dicked teenage boy
was sweating. it was a hot summer night.
in fact, it was nearly midnight.
he was taking a chance being
here in the barn at this hour, naked,
but, well, his parents knew he
had projects going on in the barn
nearly all the time, and weren't too
surprised when he left the house
and went down there to the barn
at all hours.
the sexy naked athletic big-dicked teenage boy
picked up another bale of hay, lifted it
over his shoulders, and threw it
up against the wall. it hit 12 feet up,
almost exactly where the other hay bale
had hit. "dang," he said. "if this is
ever an olympic event, i'll do real good."
he was sweaty all over. he could feel
the sweat dripping off his balls.
his pubic hair was wet.

the tip of his dick felt cool
from the sweat that ran onto it,
and then dripped off. it began
to rain. it thudded against
the tin roof.
god,
the sexy naked athletic big-dicked teenage boy
loved being out here in the barn, in
the rain. his big dick got instantly
hard, he could almost hear the "sproinnng" sound of
his dick as it sprung to fully-erect, just like that.
the rain pounded on the roof of the barn
and he stood there pumping his big hard dick.
he was standing near the wall.
the thunder went boom.
he started spurting cum.
the first blob of cum hit the wall, 12 feet up.
the second blob, not so high,
but, dern close.
after he spurted the last little
droplet, which in fact just
dribbled onto his toes,
the sexy naked athletic big-dicked teenage boy
stood there like a wild-eyed maniac,
and thought everything through,
right to the scent of ozone,
the plight of the lonely spaghetti,
heaped high with a stringy yellow mass
of steaming parmesan cheese.

greasy tip

the clatter of tiny reindeer hooves awoke
the sexy naked big-dicked teenage boy.
it was christmas eve, and, despite
the promise of new clothes and
telecommunications gadgetry,
all the sexy naked big-dicked teenage boy
was really thinking about was
his own big hard throbbing dick, and,
um, er, well,
this did give him cause to wonder:
was that sound
over his head
actually
the clatter of tiny reindeer hooves?
on the roof over his bed?
the sexy naked big-dicked teenage boy
threw back the covers and
got out of bed, his big dick
hard and throbbing and projecting
out a substantial distance in
front of the rest of him.
he heard clatters and bings and
bangs, and, when he went
to his window, he discovered that all 8 of
the tiny little reindeer were now
peeking in the window at him.
they had big brown eyes,
and the sleigh to which
they were tethered
kind of drifted magically
out behind them. it was empty,
save for a mound of packages.
no santa claus.
the sexy naked big-dicked teenage boy
was so alarmed and surprised and
intrigued, that, just for a moment,
his big hard dick went soft.

then, the 8 little reindeer
drifted on down
to the ground, and then
santa bounded out the front
door, jumped into the sleigh,
and
off the whole assembly went,
up into the air, just like a
disappearing UFO.
the sexy naked big-dicked teenage boy
stood staring out the window.
he was pretty excited.
in fact, his big
dick went instantly hard again, in less
than the blink of an eye.
the sexy naked big-dicked teenage boy
stood there in front of his window,
his big dick throbbing, begging
for attention.
and, as the glowing clock on
his bedside table skittered toward
christmas day,
the sexy naked big-dicked teenage boy
tugged on his big smooth dick,
and,
when he began to spurt cum,
the candy canes on the mantle piece
downstairs in the living room
turned pure white, drained
entirely,
of all that worrisome
red.
later, when the
smoke alarm went off,
turned out just to
be a grilled cheese sandwich,
glowing like yesterday,
or the day before,
when

the sky was a bead of stars,
and the moon,
just a little pip.

who ya like better? gauguin? or caravaggio?

when sitting in warm yogurt, virginia, and
gravitating toward the moon,
the two sexy naked big-dicked boys
looked around their college dorm room,
and were delighted with the collection
of stuff that they had crammed into their
snug little room: balls of newspaper,
and wads of string, old brightly painted
tennis shoes, and dried ears of
corn collected from halloween
corn fields, at midnight,
last week, during an especially
nice drunken foray into the
surrounding countryside.
the two sexy naked big-dicked boys
were college sophomores, majoring
in art and art history.
the two boys were in love with
each other. and they
kind of liked being
here in warm yogurt, virginia,
and they kind of hated it,
too, boonies-backwoods
college in the middle
of the mountains, in
the middle of nowhere.
now, though,
the two sexy naked big-dicked boys
were just as happy as they could be,
sitting here on the floor facing
each other. they were each masturbating,
each boy tugging on his own
big sturdy dick, and
watching each other do that.
they were kind of drunk,
they were happy with the

stuff they'd crammed into
their little dorm room,
and
they enjoyed watching each
other jerk off.
they were good-looking boys,
and enjoyed each other's being that way.
"tyrannosaurus rex was sure
a mean ole dinosaur,"
said the first boy.
"oh i don't know,"
said the other boy. "i suspect
he was just hungry all the time."
"that'd do it all right,"
said the first boy.
they sat there tugging
on their big smooth cocks,
almost ready to spurt cum,
it was easy to tell. their
balls were pulled up
real tight against their
sweet sexy bodies, and
the skin of their cocks
was so tight it seemed
to be made of stretched
and gleaming cellophane.
"gonna do it," said
the first sexy naked big-dicked boy,
and he began spurting cum,
big gobs of it,
up and back, splatting
his chest and belly.
"might as well,"
said the second sexy naked big-dicked boy,
and he, too, spurted big gooey gobs of
cum, up onto his own taut sexy chest
and flat sweaty belly.

then, "ahhhhhh," said both boys,
at exactly the same time.
the dried ears of corn, the balls
of newspaper, wads of
string, the mounds of
brightly painted tennis shoes.
the two sexy naked big-dicked young men
sitting naked on the floor,
the air smelling of cum.
ah, autumn in warm yogurt, virginia.
ah, the taste of fall.

frequency of intercourse

i am the barbarian battering at the gate.
my teeth are sharp, and covered with
gargle. my fingernails are ready to
tear civilization into tattered shreds,
and fill in the gaps with pauses.
i will demolish existing power structures.
i will smash approval ratings.
i will tie up sexy squirming young men
and manipulate their genitals for my
own satisfaction. i will jerk them
off and watch them spurt their semen
even if they say that's what they
do not want.
i will be so gentle they will almost
be deceived.
lulled into pleasure.
i will fast when they feast.
i will turn the message of fear
into the message of terror.
and, of course, i will
pour alcohol (probably vodka) into
the cherry smash, and
insist on inebriation standards.
they will be quite, and quietly,
generous. booze will be
insistently available.
there will be no such thing as too drunk. non-
existent the concept of
too lush to go on, marching to
victory, oh, the squeal of
triumph, the roar
of insipid praise.

brine

when white water is spilling into the ocean
and chicken guts are spread across the land,
then is the moment when the sexy naked big-dicked young
man
pauses, and reflects, and
eats a hamburger, and walks across the
street to where the boy he loves
sits waiting, and
the two of them spend about 5 hours
in bed, not sleeping, just
touching and groping and sliming
each other in wonderfully sexual
ways.
**

then, spent and contented,
the sexy naked big-dicked young man
leaves the bed of the boy he loves.
then, the sexy naked big-dicked young man
goes off to
work: painting, and sorting, and priming.
**

the boy he loves whimpers, and
waits for the return of the man that he loves.
**

missionary zeal overtakes the land,
and primordial commencement exercises
graduate everyone who
completed the course work.
**

later that week,
the sexy naked big-dicked young man
and the boy he loves
head off to the wilderness,
fireside chats, roasting
marshmallows, sitting
naked by the fire, heating

their sexy naked lightly-furred balls
by the gentle flame of midnight—
the roar of the ocean is louder
now, and almost upstages
a dinner for two.
**

so, behold the power
of a crater on the moon,
the werewolf in
the cistern, rotting
quietly.

point of order

when walking the walter,
be sure and don't rush him.
give him plenty of time. if
he needs to stop to pee, for
god's sake! let
him stop to pee!
try not to stare at his dick,
though, no matter how
beautiful his dick is.
the walter's quite shy.
if you stare at his dick,
that'll just make the walter cringe.
the walter just hates
having his big beautiful dick stared at.
**

when letting the walter run
free in the back yard,
generally he'll take off
all his clothes if no one's
around.
the walter is beautiful,
sexy, big-dicked, just really quite
beautiful. the walter's
eyes are ice-blue,
and his snappy little
butt is firm, tight, and
muscular.
**

at night,
the walter often escapes
from the back yard,
and runs away to the
local college track,
where he'll run
laps and run laps
and run laps until

he's bathed in sweat.
he runs naked
on that track,
and, in the summertime
heat,
sweat drips from
his sweet sexy body,
and lands
in big wet plops
on the special foot-sensitive pavement
of the oh-so-foot-friendly tarmac
of that sweat-sexy college track.
**

the walter longs
to be on the college
track team,
but he's so brilliant,
he seems destined
only for physics,
or biochemistry,
whichever has the
most nutritional value,
and offers
the biggest reward
for his happy healthy, tho slightly
panting, great big
pink-tongued return.

the ruins of pompeii

considering the state of anxiety, the
suspension of disbelief is a mercy.
warblers on the back fence stretch
their tiny wings and sing notes
of ancient evolutionary rhythms,
the jars of pickles on the
back shelf in the kitchen dating
back to the early 1900s, perhaps
even further. yet, they're
still a lovely shade of
dark green. if only the
blustering wind would settle
down for a while, and
bother somebody else,
perhaps the hairy ass
of a muscular woodworker
in the throes of creativity,
he likes to work stark naked,
his ass hair blowing back
and forth in the noon-day
sun, as the wooden trellis
that he is building
takes shape, and rises
into the sky like the
overbearing yammering of
a jillion cicadas,
waiting their turn
for sex and sunlight,
after all those
years in the mulch.

the realm of logic

while the water was rushing down the washboard belly
of the sexy big-dicked young man who was wearing
only a baggy red swimsuit,
fourteen massive walruses ate hundreds perhaps even
thousands of pounds of fresh fish flesh,
and
slimy scales stuck to their whiskers.
meanwhile,
the sexy big-dicked young man who was wearing
only a baggy red swimsuit
stepped out of the shower,
and
disappeared into
the wilds of wisconsin,
never to be seen again.
the walrus population
has been in decline ever since.

thunderstorms in the afternoon

while in the wildnerness, eat vanilla soft-serve
ice cream. it's the only sensible choice.
talk to the birds. slither with the snakes.
express yourself in polysyllabic hyperbole.
when you have to pee, drench the soil, not
the moss. order your dinner well before the
5 o'clock rush.
**

such were the thoughts of
the sexy naked big-dicked young man
as he awoke in the morning,
stretching and yawning and scratching his balls.
the phrase
"order your dinner well before the
5 o'clock rush" made him chuckle,
all alone in his room. he didn't
remember WHAT the heck he'd been
dreaming, but there was this string
of words slobbering around on
his wet pink tongue. he did
recall an image of himself
standing all alone in the
forest,
wishing he could go home,
but,
enjoying that super-soft vanilla ice cream
so much he thought he should
never leave the forest, or
that ice cream.
the sexy naked big-dicked young man
yawned and stretched and scratched his
balls once again. he still had a few
minutes, so he threw back
the covers and lay there
on his back and had a
nice leisurely jerk-off, did

it nice and slow, spurted
a big glob of cum, didn't even
wipe it off his belly before
he headed into the shower,
just stood there
letting the hot water wash
over him, wash the cum
down the drain. golly,
he was in a good mood.
something had to give.

your eyes look funny today

the moo goo gai pan of love is
the spicy sauce of dreamsville,
the textured platinum of
corduroy pants that cling
to the crotches of beautiful
big-dicked boys. the smear
of love jelly on the
tops of the sheets is
but an indicator
of the slobbery appetites
sometimes engendered
by the pitty-patting
hearts of those
who are obsessed
with each other's
minds and souls
and bodies, and not
necessarily in that
order, either. the odor
of love is
sometimes
so thick with the
scent of sex
it'll make a
grown football player
blush. sometimes,
it's just the wacky
scent of
dimestore perfume.
inhaled, or licked,
it's something
for the tastebuds
to fight over.

purity is a thing of virtue

the squeaky wheel gets the grease.
then how about the squeaky dick?
how about the squeaky Zygote?
when things squeak, they should get
the grease. shouldn't they?
**

the lean sinewy big-dicked sexy young man
slathers a lot of vaseline on his
dick when he's jerking off.
this doesn't stop all sound,
but it makes a smooth slippery
sloshy kind of sound
instead of
a sharp painful-sounding
flesh-whapping-flesh kind of sound.
**

another little
Zygote goes right on growing.
**

the
wright brothers'
very first flight was
on a north carolina
island— it
disturbed the sea gulls
so much
they've never
quite
recovered.

for 100% accuracy

when buying
leopard paint,
don't forget
the
"grass-stain green"
for
the
paws.

a clean aquarium

the cruikshank of debilitation lends
itself to a perversely-smattered spatter
of reason, amorphous dreams
of misspent youthful indiscretion,
the wind in the willows sings
of "strip & fuck" while the
textbooks say study aristotle, and
prometheus lifts his muscular
arms to reveal
his torrid turgid cum-spurting
dick, the vulture that
gnaws out his liver
dripping bilious ooze from its
delicately hooked beak.
**

when the grass turned a brightly
delicate pink of green
in the forced warmth of
spring, the blue-eyed
big-dicked boy found himself
weeping at darn near
anything, spurting cum
at the drop of a
hat, and swallowing
honeysuckle nectre and bee's wax
cascade until he was
kissed passionately on the
lips by his best friend gregory,
and the two of them lay
in bed together for 3 days
solid and touched each other
in every way possible, sexual
carnal and spiritual emotional,
love was the sticky essence
of palpitory delight, and
glucose-fructose the
gooey projectile sustenance
of raw rampant gustatory
need.

copperheads and rattlesnakes

sitting on the couch wearing only his socks,
the sexy big-dicked teenage boy
sprouted a hardon and sat there
watching a sexy show on tv.
very soon,
the sexy big-dicked teenage boy
took off one sock and
put it on his dick, instead
of on his foot.
then, the sexy big-dicked teenage boy
sat there on the couch wearing only
a sock on his left foot,
and a sock on his big hard dick.
the tv show got a little bit sexier
and
the sexy big-dicked teenage boy
felt a little bit hornier
and
he was soon playing with his
dick through the sock that covered it.
he was patting his dick and caressing it
and wrapping his fingers around it
and tugging on it quite gently
while he watched the sexy tv
show while wearing only one sock
on his left foot
and the other sock on his dick.
soon,
he spurted a big sloppy wad of hot
gooey cum into the toe of
the sock that was covering his dick.
he smiled with pleasure
and spread his butt cheeks and kind
of rubbed his tight pink asshole against the
cushion of the couch.
then,

the sexy big-dicked teenage boy
took the sock off his dick
and the other sock off his left
foot
and he walked into
the bathroom and tossed
the two socks into the
laundry hamper.
then he stood there naked
staring at himself in the mirror.
he really was good-looking,
and it was nice to be aware of himself
good-looking and big-dicked
and just a general appealing
presence in the sexual nature
of the universe. "i'm a good
addition to all
of it, everything," he assured himself.
then,
still naked,
the sexy big-dicked teenage boy
went back to the couch and
sat down and watched some
more of the sexy tv show.
he was feeling kind of hungry,
but when the nicest-looking girl on the show
took off her bra,
he delayed his trip
to the kitchen for a few moments
more,
and
the taste of the ham
he hoped to soon have in his mouth
quickly became
torture.
he could practically hear the
pig screaming as it

died so inelegantly,
the slaughterhouse floor
a goddamn bloody mess.

be sure and wash behind your ears, too

wail and weep if you must, but
don't expect that corn to harvest itself.
strap on your sturdiest clothes,
put your cock protector firmly in place
if you must,
but you get out there, and you harvest that corn.
the fact that you are
a sexy big-dicked good-looking young man
will not get you out of that corn harvest
this year, just as it didn't
get your ass out of it
last year.
you tried to get out of it last year, too,
didn't ya?
but did that work?
i don't think so.
so,
get yourself out there,
you
sexy big-dicked good-looking young man,
and harvest that goddamn corn.
i'm counting on you.
the nation is counting on you.
heck, the whole fuckin' world is
counting on you.
then, once you're done with that
for this year,
get yourself on back in the house,
take off your clothes,
and relax.
you've earned it.
hell, jerk off if you want.
you've earned that, too.
and i'll watch you do it, just to make
sure the your technique is good,
up to speed, that sort of thing.

we can't have you floudering around
without any guidance at all, now
can we.
we tried that before.
and look where that went.

once again, autumn arrives

the sexy naked big-dicked teenage boy stood
around squirting raw grapes into his mouth.
it had been a good harvest, and the
grapes this year were especially sweet.
he squirted one grape after another into
his mouth, and he swallowed everything that
went into his mouth, seeds and all.
he flung all the eviscerated
grape skins onto the ground,
and there were soon a lot of them,
wet droopy purple husks,
all around his sexy naked feet.
**

his step-brother came out of the house
and told him to stop eating grapes,
and to put on some clothes, for
a change.
he didn't really mean it, though.
**

the step-brother was hunky and
sexy and often wore nothing himself.
**

they had a unique relationship.
not exactly incest, but
something kinda close to it.
**

the sexy naked big-dicked teenage boy
and his hunky step-brother often
watched pornographic movies together,
while jerking themselves off,
but they thought that that didn't really count.
**

they are probably right.
still, though,
it's only natural to wonder...
**

on full-moon nights when
the wolves are howling
outside their window, they
sometimes sleep together.
for comfort, and
warmth.

indulgence is the sincerest form of saying yes

Jamie Bell (star of BILLY ELLIOT and THE CHUMSCRUBBER
and MISTER FOE), are you secretly reading my poetry?
Jamie Bell, you beautiful big-dicked young man, are
you secretly reading my poetry
about beautiful big-dicked young men,
beautiful big-dicked young men just like you?
**

Jamie Bell, i hope you're flattered, and
not creeped out, that i can so easily
picture you totally naked, lying on
your back atop your bed, and you
are so gently oh you are
so gently tugging on your big
hard smooth dick. when you spurt
cum, your eyes flash like
mystical sparks and your
sweet charming crooked little grin peeks
through your wet tongue-licked
lips.
**

Jamie Bell, are you secretly
reading my poetry about
beautiful big-dicked young men
who do the sort of things
that i imagine you do,
in the privacy of your
own room, on your bed,
alone, experiencing
the joy you experience
at touching your beautiful
body in the respectful
and reverent ways that
you touch your nipples,
and dick, and balls,
and let your fingers
linger over just the

tips of your untrimmed
pubic hair.
you are
a wild man, there
all alone, thrashing
about, dreaming of
my sweet
sexy poems,
and me.

springsummer winterfall

the sexy naked sophomore college boy and the
scrawny skinny naked freshman college boy
are sitting in their dorm room on
the bottom bunk, legs crossed, facing each other.
they are eating crackers.
the scrawny skinny naked freshman college boy
has sprouted quite a nice big hardon, and
the sexy naked sophomore college boy
comments: "you've got a hardon."
the scrawny skinny naked freshman college boy
replies: "these are certainly excellent crackers,
aren't they?"
then, with almost the accompanying "SPROING!" sound,
the sexy naked sophomore college boy sprouts
a nice big hardon, too.
the two boys sit there eating their crackers
and staring at each other's hardons.
"JERK-OFF BREAK!!" they both shout in
perfect unison.
and that's exactly what they do,
the sexy naked sophomore college boy and the
scrawny skinny naked freshman college boy,
sitting there across from each other
on the bottom bunk, jerking themselves off
until they spurt cum all over their own
naked chests and bellies.
then, with one graceful, seemingly pre-rehearsed
motion, they each grab a handful of tissues
from the nearby tissue box, and wipe
themselves off.
"well," says
the sexy naked sophomore college boy to the
scrawny skinny naked freshman college boy,
"back to the crackers?"
"they are tasty, aren't they?" says
the scrawny skinny naked freshman college boy,
"and salty, too."
"we like salt," say the two boys together.
"we do we do we do."

broom handle

my prayer robe is open,
and my dick is sticking out.
elsewhere in the house,
water is running,
and no doubt the bathtub will
soon overflow.
and yet,
my prayer robe is open,
and my dick is sticking out.
the wildfires that sweep
through the canyons
have charred thousands
of trees. small birds
are in flames.
little whispers of
change are on the lips
of the hopeful.
oh, heck yeah, my prayer robe is open,
and my dick is sticking out.
melodies on the
radio remind me of
torrid times in
the old dorm room,
just me and my roommate,
his face was so sweet,
his cock was so big.
now, my prayer robe is open,
and parted wide across
my naked chest.
the tip of my dick
is cold,
the room is drafty,
and the knowledge
that i'm about to
turn
59 years old

has already knocked my
socks off.
yep, naked
all over, bare toes,
too, just like
the old
neighborhood,
when i was 5 years old and
stepped
on honey bees and
regretted everything,
having no thoughts for
tomorrow; as i recall,
my only immediate
concern was
the pain.

the fountain of youth

the train
left at 7 a.m.
**

everybody aboard was unconcerned.
**

they'd eaten cranberries for breakfast,
and rejected the canaries.
**

passengers
often
sniff at stuff they don't eat,
but could, if they
wanted to.
**

pond scum is really just algae.

then get out of the kitchen

the boy with the plutonium dick
has eyes of fire,
dreams of 4th of july,
believes in total sexual conquest.
he wants slaves.
lots of them.
**

all alone in
his room, its walls
covered with aluminum foil,
the boy with the plutonium dick
practices his aim,
perfects trajectory masturbation and
spatters the paper target
bullseye with his own
cum. he's got a good
aim. the center of
the target bursts into
flame, then evaporates,
when his cum hits it.
this always
makes him chuckle.
**

the boy with the plutonium dick
fucks his best friend paul
right up the ass.
paul likes the heat.
and can take it.
paul's very good-looking.
and paul's got a great ass,
in spite of the burnmarks.
**

the boy with the plutonium dick
kisses paul tenderly after
he fucks paul, and then
the boy with the plutonium dick

sucks paul off, as paul
whimpers with
sexual ecstasy, there
on the muddy leaf-strewn ground,
for they like to do
it in the woods,
and the occasional forest fire,
well, that's just too bad.

that's his summer diet

the plethora of wild pigs wandering around
in the desert helped convince
the sexy naked big-dicked college boy,
home on summer break,
that he needed to eat more pork.
and soooooo....
the sexy naked big-dicked college boy
got out his bow and arrow,
and practiced until he
could hit a nickel at 100 yards,
and then he started killing wild
pigs.
the sexy naked big-dicked college boy
was really good at it, too.
he hunted at dusk,
when it was cool, and
all the pigs were out rooting
around for their
bedtime snack, and, after he got
a nice big one, he
butchered it on the spot,
cooked what he wanted over
an open fire, and then sat
there his legs spread wide
gently warming his balls
by the pork-scented flames.
once the fire was out,
he left the remaining pig carcass
for whatever wanted to eat it—
coyotes and foxes by night,
and, at day,
out came the vultures to
finish off the job.
**

every night, on the way
home from his naked pig killing and
pork feasting, he stopped
long enough to

jerk himself off
beside a big old spikey cactus.
he always spurted his cum
onto the base of the cactus,
and the cactus seemed
to appreciate the extra
nutrients that it was receiving.
**

then,
after jerking off,
the sexy naked big-dicked college boy
walked on home, to his parents' house,
the place he was living this summer,
and, before entering the house,
he put on a shirt, shoes, and
pair of pants he kept hidden
in the outbuilding behind
the house. there, too,
he left his bow and arrow.
"hello folks!" he always said
to his parents, as he
entered the house, as they sat
on the couch watching late-nite
tv. "nice to see ya!" he said to them.
"nice to see you, too," they
said, catching the waft of
smoke and cooked wild pig,
the general look of
untamability in his
sparkling and dazzling
eyes. that was about it,
though, the extent
of their conversation,
as he headed off to
the shower, and
then bed, and
sleep.

nesting

two cute big-dicked young men
climb into bed together.
they pull up the covers.
"good night" they say.
**

a moment of silence follows.
**

soon, they are asleep.
**

in the middle of the night,
though,
one guy pretends to remain asleep
while the other guy is busily
jerking off beside him.
**

the bed shakes subtly, rhythmically; there's
a sudden squeak. then silence.
tires screech on
the road outside, and once again,
silence.

sometimes, time pitty-pats on quiet feet

it was unlikely that he would be overheard, but
still, though, the sexy young man
was always very very quiet when he
was masturbating. he lay on his
back, surrounded by dozens of others
who slept around him. it was on
the maximum security ward of
a psychiatric hospital. a handtowel
dangled from the head of the metal bed.
most of the other patients seemed to be
medicated to a far greater level
than he was. they slept the sleep
that would not end until they
were awaken by the orderlies
in the morning. him, though,
he wasn't as heavily medicated.
he guessed he wasn't as "sick"
as those with whom he was
surrounded. in the middle
of the night, looking at
the bars that covered the windows,
he felt the urgency of his
hard dick under the sheets,
and he masturbated into
the towel that he withdrew
oh so quietly from the head
of his bed, and, after
he came, he returned the
towel to its position where
it dried before morning.
he always wondered if his
towel was subsequently examined
by someone on the staff
for evidence
of masturbatory activity.
but, if it was, he was

never told about it.
when released from the
psychiatric hospital,
the sexy young man
for months and months
maintained his habit
of silent of so
very very silent masturbatory
activity. then, one night,
all alone in his own little
apartment, he decided
to groan and grunt and howl
as much as possible during
the whole procedure— just
be as theatric as possible.
and so he writhed and
moaned and groaned and grunted
naked sweaty on his back
on the bed tugging with
great force and zest and zeal on
his great big smooth hard cock,
shaking the bed, rattling
the mattress and when
he spurted cum, he
howled like a wolf.
then, quiet again,
he lay there smiling
with such a silly grin
on his handsome face,
he felt almost sheepish.
"baaaaa" he said
softly, and then he
burst into sweet
gentle throaty laughter.
"baaa baaa baaa"
he said again. and then,
he giggled so

charmingly, it was
almost as though
he had never actually
been sick,
but, if he had been sick
(and ok, yeah, he
most certainly was), well,
those days were gone,
and, now, relaxed and
beautiful naked sweaty
on the soft
white sheets, wiggling
his toes, he
was quite sure those
days were behind him,
and that none of it would
ever happen again.

everybody deserves at least one

candy lay melting on the floor, dripping down
the front of the stove, as
the sexy skinny teenage boy
walked around naked in the kitchen,
a drippy candy-covered wooden spoon in one hand,
a long glass-tube-shaped cooking thermometer
in the other hand. the sexy skinny teenage boy
had been having fun, cooking there at
home all alone, after deciding to make
a batch of candy from scratch:
butterscotch, with chocolate swirled
throughout. the kitchen smelled
wonderful, as he walked around
naked with the drippy spoon in one hand
and the cooking thermometer in the other hand.
and, now that dozens of delicious-looking blobs
of candy were resting on the wax-paper-covered
cooking pans scattered all around
on the kitchen countertops, and the
air was filled with the scent of
warm butterscotch and chocolate, the
sexy skinny naked teenage boy found
that he had sprouted quite a hardon,
there in the kitchen, surrounded
by all that candy.
he put down the spoon. he put down
the thermometer. he
grabbed a blob of the warm
candy from one of
the wax-paper-covered pans, and he
put that blob of warm candy onto his
tongue, letting it kind of
sit there, melting into the
slobbery pinkness. he looked
down at his hot beautiful throbbing
dick. he looked at the spots

of melty candy lying on the floor,
and at the
drips that ran down the front
of the stove. then, without
even touching his dick, he
spurted out several large gushes
of cum, and his orgasm
was so good his cum
landed about 5 feet away
from him, spotty on the
floor, mingling with some
of the candy drippings.
"wow" he said, right outloud
there in the kitchen.
"perfect day."

banana yellow

when smearing water-color paint all over
the body of a sexy naked young man (a
young man such as Andrew Garfield— maybe
you've seen him
in the movie THE SOCIAL NETWORK or
NEVER LET ME GO),
anyhow, when smearing water-color paint
all over Andrew Garfield's (a sexy
naked young man) body,
i'd go for the nipples
first, then
the sunburst around his
bellybutton.
his scrotum would
be next,
and then the
shaft of his cock.
each of these would
be painted a different
color.
and, the more he giggled,
the more i would,
too.

i think he said his name was "lucky"

for his halloween costume,
the sexy big-dicked young man decided
to go naked. in other words, he decided he'd
"dress up" as a nudist.
this thought amused the sexy big-dicked young man
very much,
and, the first door he knocked on,
a young woman answered.
"trick or treat," said
the sexy naked big-dicked young man.
he held out a little brown paper sack,
and waited for his treat.
the young woman slammed the door in his face.
he turned and walked down the sidewalk.
very soon, a police car showed up.
two cops hurried over to the
sexy naked big-dicked young man,
and one of the cops wrapped a blanket
around him.
"you're under arrest," said the cop who
had wrapped him up with the blanket.
"indecent exposure."
"but it's halloween," said the
sexy naked big-dicked young man,
"and this is my costume. i'm 'dressed
up' as a nudist. get it?"
and then the young man
laughed, quite charmingly.
"yeah yeah," said the other cop. "very funny.
but you're STILL under arrest for indecent exposure."
and so the two cops and the sexy big-dicked young man
who was wrapped up in the blanket
drove to the police station/jail.
they booked the sexy big-dicked young man
and issued him some jail clothes and
put him a cell and told him to

get dressed.
the sexy big-dicked young man
refused. in fact, he threw off the blanket,
and stood there sexy, naked, big-dicked,
with a full horny erection that suddenly looked,
in fact, like it was made entirely out of
bone, and then encrusted with
brittle knobby chunks of tortoise shell.
there then ensued what seemed to be
a general melting and fusing of flesh,
and the creature that
the sexy naked big-dicked young man
had become kicked out the bars
of the cell's window, unfurled
a pair of wings, and flew off into the
starry night-time sky.
"happy halloween," were the parting words
the two cops heard, as the goosebumps
seized them, and covered their
pale municipal flesh.

political moderate

the smog and fog of everyday disenlightenment
stultifies, paralyzes, disembowels, putrifies:
terrifies.
do you believe in nihilism?
i believe in nihilism.
do you believe in nihilism?
i believe in nihilism.
but do you really believe in nihilism?
yes, i REALLY do believe in nihilism.
a cute naked young man, spreading
land 'o' lakes butter on his
smooth lightly-furred balls and on
his big hard dick
because he wants to find out
how it feels when he uses
land 'o' lakes butter as
a lubricant during masturbation:
how does he fit into the scheme
of things? how does he fit
into the big picture?
his 10-20-30 minutes of
pure butter-lubricated pleasure
are then punctuated by hours
and hours of, the, dull, the
ordinary, the routine: where,
exactly, does all that fit?
the nothingness of most all of
it all but
overwhelms him. he sinks
into bouts of pure nasty depression
that span between each session
of pure sexual bliss.
he learns that land 'o' lakes
ain't a bad lubricant, but
vaseline is still king
of that domain.

he learns to believe in
nihilism, and his dick,
in nihilism, and spurting cum.
mood swings go from one to
the other. there is nothing
in between. years later,
the sight of a stick of
butter still turns him on.
ignites sparks at his
dickhead, initiates tingling
in the pink deepness of
his thin delicate pee-hole.
the rest is murkiness, smog,
and fog, the wetness of
a wishy-washy summer mist,
can't decide if it's rain
or fog or something in between,
as if there is any in-between,
as if such a thing
were, finally, possible.

soul

while the cattle are lowing,
two big strapping farmboys are up in
the hay-loft fucking each other.
a few minutes later, the two big strapping farmboys
lie there naked beside each other
staring up at the roof and feeling
the warm summer air rushing
across their hot shimmery sweaty bodies
from the two big windows at
either end of the hay-loft.
the cattle continue lowing.
"good night for it," says one sexy farmboy to
the other.
"yep," says the other sexy farmboy. "sure is."
then they kiss each other big-time wet and sloppy,
tongues down the throat, the whole bit.
the cattle go right on lowing.
the breeze goes right on rushing from one big open
window to the other big open window.
"let's do it again" says one sexy farmboy.
"ok" says the other sexy farmboy.
and so the two sexy naked farmboys fuck,
and one of 'em spurts
cum up the other's ass, and at the exact
same time one sexy farmboy is spurting cum
up the other's ass, the sexy farmboy who's
getting fucked is so turned on he's spurting
cum himself—goes splat splat splat right
there onto the hay-covered floor of the loft.
"god" they both say at that exact same moment when
both of them are spurting cum. "oh god."
the cattle are lowing.
the breeze moves through the loft.
the two sexy naked farmboys roll apart
and stand up and stare at each other
naked and hot and sweaty.
"god," they both say. "lordy."

scholarship

mistakes were made.
demerits were handed out.
bad grades were given.
boy butts were bared and spanked.
there was an atmosphere of sparks and
combs.
plumes of cum jetted through the
night air.
restlessness spoke
in muffled voices, smoked furtive cigarettes,
sneaked a bit of booze.
sometimes companionship looked more
like love than self-preservation.
corporality was not without its rewards,
naked there among the boulders, hiding
from the powers that inflicted
lessons, lectures, books, and
pre-set computer screens.
when dicks were bared, and
cum allowed its natural channels
of flow, talk was barely necessary,
though the use of dirty words was
found to enhance the whole experience.
back in the classrooms,
more demerits were handed out,
more bad grades were given, and
more boy butts were bared and spanked.
anyone even smirked, well,
it was chaucer for them, and
lots of it. shakespeare was administered
in
the severest situations,
and was found to elicit the
most nausea, and therefore,
it was thought,
the best hope of
change.
mike played the clarinet.
and glen practiced al.

fly

mostly i like to dwell on the quiet
moments of sexy male movie stars. for instance,
i can easily picture a relaxed conversation
between john stamos and jake gyllenhaal in
a secluded mountain sauna—no one around
except them—they are sitting across from
one another in the sauna totally naked,
no towels, and they are having
an honest heart-to-heart talk about
the infinite respect they have for
each other's bodies, that the male
body as a work of art has been in vogue
for centuries, and will never go out
of vogue, and as they talk about the
beauty of the male body, they get
around to the good-lookingness of
each other, and become more and
more aware, that, as they sit
there naked, legs spread, talking
to each other, they have each
gotten a hardon. as john stamos talks,
his own hard smooth cock jounces a bit, along
with the syllables, and, as jake gyllenhaal
talks, his own hard smooth cock jounces along
with his own syllabic utterances and cadences, and,
as both their voices become softer and sexier
and more introspective, they
sit there across from each
other talking, and out of
the blue, they just start
spurting cum, without
even touching their own cocks
or each other's cocks, they
just spurt cum and spurt cum
and spurt cum, and all the
while talk calmly and intimately

about the historic artistic focus
on the beauty of a sexy nude man and
about how they are each quietly aware that
each of them is a sexy good-looking man,
too, their shape and form and
general aura not unlike that
of excellent naked male forms from
the past.
**

the aroma of their own freshly spurted cum infuses the
hot moist air with a ripe sensual and murky muskiness,
suffused with the near-praeternatural intimacy of the moment.
**

naked john stamos and
naked jake gyllenhaal sit there in the secret sauna,
their legs spread, their big smooth dicks
still semi-turgid, their cum puddled
on the sauna floor boards and on the sauna benches and,
just a bit,
on their respective bellies, too.
**

"good conversation is the spice
of life isn't it," says jake gyllenhaal.
"indeed it is," says john stamos.
**

steam hisses from the steam-maker, and
outside, snow begins to fall.
**

the earth spins and spins, and,
inside that sauna, i'm just a bit woozy myself.
**

"i masturbate first thing every morning," says jake gyllenhaal.
"hey me too" says john stamos. "me too."

be

two sexy high-school boys have skipped school today
and are now standing naked
on the big smooth gray rock that overlooks
the surface of a warm gentle secluded pond,
only a few feet below.
"1 2 3 go," says one of the sexy high-school boys,
and they both dive into the pond,
swim a while, then swim over to
the shallow area on the other side, splash around,
end up hugging each other tight, and kissing each other on the
lips, and grabbing onto each other's big
sturdy cocks, and jerking each other
off, there in the shallows on the other side of
the pond. then they hug each other again,
kiss, suck on each other's tongues a bit,
and then swim back onto the other side
of the pond and
climb out onto the warm smooth gray
rock that they had jumped off of.
they lie down on their backs side
by side and stare up at the sky.
"i'm glad we skipped school today," says
one of the sexy high-school boys.
"me too," says the other sexy high-school boy.
about 20 birds are singing from all
around the pond. the sunlight is warm,
friendly, and pretty dern spectacular.

gorilla architecture

"refry the beans on the doorstep of darkness"
and
"cherish the fallen angels, for they are
often the most beautiful" —
these were the thoughts
that the sexy big-dicked young man
was having as he was watching
the birds migrate, and,
as he watched them through
the little tiny itty bitty interwoven
holes of his screened-in porch,
he kept saying to himself,
"refry the beans on the doorstep of darkness"
and
"cherish the fallen angels, for they are
often the most beautiful" — until,
the certainty of his own
madness loomed like
a twisting clothesline
on the horizon,
and even the
turnip that was sucking on
his dick
could no longer distract
him from the certainty
of orgasmic
introspectivity,
the yearning of his
pants to slither back
up his ankles, and, at
the very least, cover up the
knees.

a rather odd saturday afternoon

so i'm taking a nap
and suddenly the aging Olympian Mark Spitz
crawls into bed with me
and his hands are all over me— embarrassingly so,
actually, since i'm no spring chicken anymore myself,
and things, have well, sagged, etc., but his
hands are nonetheless all over me and i say to him
"i'm pretty much over-the-hill, body-wise, and
what do you see in me?" and Mark Spitz replies
"i really dig your poetry. it's hot. i like
your poetry a lot."
and he rubs his hands all over my skinny not-very-muscular
chest and explores my belly button with one of
his finger tips.
**

my hubby walks into the
bedroom at that moment. my hubby is not amused.
my hubby does not like Mark Spitz being
in bed with me. my hubby
says to Mark Spitz "get out of here right now!"
and to me, my hubby says, "and i'll have a LOT to say
to YOU later, buster."
my hubby has never ever called me "buster" and
his word choice is alarming.
**

Mark Spitz says to my hubby "i won 7 Olympic Gold Medals
in swimming, and this entitles me to certain
things in life, one of which is getting
to rub my hands all over Carl Miller Daniels' body
if that's what i want to do. Carl's poems are
great. i really dig Carl's poems, and I really dig Carl."
**

my hubby says "FUCK! YOU! MARK! FUCKIN! SPITZ!!!
GET THE HELL OUT OF HERE RIGHT NOW!!!!!"
**

Mark Spitz cops a feel to my aging but highly
excitable dick, and then he leaves, slamming

the front door behind him.
**

then it's just me and my hubby. "how the
HELL did Mark Spitz get in here?" he asks.
i really don't know the answer to that one.
"i really don't know," i say. "perhaps
the back door was unlocked?"
"hmmmm," says my hubby, a skeptical look
on his fuzzy face.
**

"ah well," i say. "at least he's gone
now, and it WAS kinda flattering, having
a great Olympic swimmer tell me he likes
my poetry."
**

"he's not even good-looking anymore,
is he?" says my hubby.
**

i quickly agree that Mark Spitz is
over-the-hill, and that he has not aged
at all gracefully. i say that Mark Spitz
is now flabby,
and things have sure sagged. also,
"he's put on weight" i add.
**

"we'll have to make sure to keep
that door locked," says my hubby.
"this has been a lesson to us."
**

"yes it has," i say. "yes it has."

toe-hold

waking up one morning,
the good-looking big-dicked sexy young man
bounded out of bed,
got in his car, and started driving.
he went far far far into
the countryside, found a
forest, parked his car,
walked into the forest,
and sat down on a rock
and thought about his life. while
he was thinking about his life,
he stripped off all his clothes
and tugged on his big hard smooth dick,
there in the forest, alone except
for the black-n-white banded
kingsnake, nestled only a
few feet away from his
naked toes.
the good-looking big-dicked sexy young man
and
the black-n-white banded kingsnake
watched each other as the
the good-looking big-dicked sexy young man
played with his own dick, and, right
after
the good-looking big-dicked sexy young man
spurted a whole bunch of cum, big gooey
gobs of it, the
black-n-white banded kingsnake said:
"pleasure is all that really matters,
isn't it?"
to which the good-looking big-dicked sexy young man
replied: "it's important, all right."
the two of them continued looking
at each other, there in the
middle of the forest,

the good-looking big-dicked sexy young man,
and
the black-n-white banded kingsnake.
then, when the
good-looking big-dicked sexy young man
said, "well, gotta go now, i'm late
for a wedding,"
the black-n-white banded kingsnake
crawled away, deeper into
the forest, profoundly disappointed
by this, his very first reptile-human inter-species
interaction.
the good-looking big-dicked sexy young man
sensed the snake's disappointment,
but, upon leaving the forest,
the good-looking big-dicked sexy young man
went to the wedding, and, while there (and
when the bride's back was turned), he
indulged in a few puzzling shenanigans with
the groom, during which, among
other things, he and the groom secretly shared
tall frothy glasses
of the most expensive champagne.

punctuating

the supposition that
life here on earth
is a few punctuation marks
of pure bliss
marking passages of
otherwise limitless boredom
and despair
is
built on a sexual model.
**

i mean, take a cute naked
big-dicked young man.
he is physically able
to spurt cum, in his
prime, 5 maybe 6 times
a day.
**

assumption: these (let's
be generous) 6 episodes
of cum-spurting in any
single given day all
occur as a result of acts of
solitary masturbation.
**

nonetheless: these 6 bouts
of cum-spurting feel
incredibly incredibly
good. he stands there
naked hot and sweaty,
blood pounding, working
his big hard smooth cock
until it spurts a few
globs of cum, and during
those seconds of cum-spurting,
he's the happiest most blissful
guy in the world.

**

then, that punctuation mark
having been laid down, the rest of
the day continues, i.e., the rest of
the passage, continues—
drearily and drearily on until
he's ready to bare his
big smooth cock and spurt
some more hot gooey drippy cum.
**

i'm just saying that
the highs of life, the
moments of pure unfettered &
passionate joy, are few
and far between.
**

if you think those are
the only things that make
a day worthwhile, for instance,
then, by comparison, the
rest of each and every day
is just one big blah expanse
of blahness.
**

people who want joy all
the time, every moment
of every day, often
go crazy hoping that
life will eventually
be that way. they often
go crazy hoping that
joy of the kind
exemplified in a
sexy good-looking
naked young man having a really
great orgasm and spurting
big gooey droplets of cum,

that kind of joy will
be permanent, all the time,
day in and day out.
**

some people are
just
wishing and wishing
and wishing life could
be like that, one extended
cum-spurt, one jolt of
pure white-hot pleasure,
every moment.
every day.
**

wishing n wishing n wishing.
**

too much wishing, that'll
drive ya crazy, too.
**

sometimes he lies on his
back, pulls his knees over
his head, aims the tip
of his dick toward his
mouth, and tries to
hit his tongue when he
cums. variety is important,
but some things, well,
they remain pretty much constant.

behavior modification

"quack quack quack," said the duck,
as
the clouds swirled ominously overhead,
and a few tentative drops of rain began to fall.
**

two sexy teenage boys were watching
a female duck get fucked by
not one, but by three male
ducks. one of the sexy teenage boys
was very angry. he thought
the male ducks were trying
to kill the female, though
he didn't know it was a female,
didn't know that the ducks
that were climbing onto
its back and nearly totally
submerging it as they fucked
it were, in fact, fucking it.
that sexy teenage boy
started throwing sticks
at the male ducks, to
try and chase them away
from the duck he thought
the male ducks were trying
to kill, though he didn't
know they were male ducks,
didn't know it was a female
duck, didn't know they
were fucking it. he thought
they were trying to kill it.
he wanted to protect it.
**

the other teenage boy
seemed to know what was going
on, though not fully.
he just told the stick-throwing boy

to stop throwing sticks
at the ducks, that
it wouldn't do any good.
"hell i'd shoot those goddamn ducks
if i had a gun," said
the stick-throwing boy.
**

eventually, all the ducks
moved away from the two
boys. the freshly-fucked
female duck, and the male
ducks that had fucked her.
**

the two sexy teenage boys
were left standing
by the river. the
two sexy teenage boys
were tense, felt odd,
angry, confused.
they had witnessed
a female duck getting fucked by
several male ducks,
but hadn't really understood
what was going on.
**

the rain began to
fall.
soon, there was no one
standing on the banks
of the river, just
the big plops of
raindrops onto
the gray flowing
surface that
moved on like
a solution to
a problem

that may not
have really
existed.

toe, and finger, nails

jamie bell
is letting me watch while he jerks himself off.
jamie bell
has been a point of fixation of mine
for many years. jamie bell is
a very sexy sweet cute handsome young actor.
i think his body is marvelous.
his crooked little smile just
sweet and endearingly sensuous.
the only time i've seen him almost
naked is in his movie "mr. foe" —
he's
almost totally naked in
that movie, but not quite totally.
anyhow i nearly lost it when
i saw that scene of him
almost naked. second only
to the scene in which
he paints red circles around
his nipples with lipstick.
**

anyhow, at this
moment i am watching jamie bell
jerk himself off, and i am
kind of
going mad
while
jamie bell is jerking himself off for me,
and,
when he spurts cum,
he smiles real big,
his eyes sparkle,
and then
he lets me smell the puddle
of cum he's left
on the bed— in fact,

he insists that
i stick my
nose right
into it,
so that he
can see his cum
on the tip
of my nose.
at this moment
it strikes me that life is certainly very strange,
but really, quite
good.

occasional fastidiousness tolerated here

susan the beekeeper keeps the bees,
and arranges the flowers.
susan has her sights set
on ralph the sexy naked big-dicked teenage boy,
but ralph the sexy naked big-dicked teenage boy seems
interested in things other than susan.
susan is a good beekeeper, and a good
arranger of flowers, and she thinks
this should be enough to
attract ralph the sexy naked big-dicked teenage boy,
but,
um,
ralph just doesn't seem attracted.
she gives ralph many bottles of honey,
and lots of vases full of lovely flowers,
but,
well,
ralph
drinks walrus blood
and puts skulls of dead animals above his fireplace.
and, left to his own devices,
ralph the sexy naked big-dicked teenage boy
eats locusts without any honey,
and
enjoys the sight of susan's flowers
composting in his compost pile.
the relationship of susan the beekeeper/flower arranger
and
ralph the sexy naked big-dicked teenage boy
isn't exactly a doomed relationship,
but, let's be realistic: it's just not
all that promising, either.
**

years later, susan the beekeeper/flower arranger,
and
ralph the sexy naked big-dicked young man,

wonder at how it ever worked out,
them married to each other now,
and
the
smell of his hot cum in the morning,
still honey to her nostrils, quivering
on the buzzing wings of wispy early-sunrise dawn.

let's go for a hike

wolfsbane the dog dregs for calm.
when the flowers bloom in springtime,
savor the situation, but not the ethics.
apart from the sanctity of human
dimensionality, there is always
the nature of precuspial pubescence,
the milk-watery dreams of
sexy naked big-dicked teenage boys,
their big smooth sturdy dicks firing
off volleys of cum like
firecrackers, but without
that much noise.
**

i was once in love with
my college roommate,
a sweet sexy member of the
college swimteam.
whenever he asked me
to go hiking with him,
my heart nearly stopped,
my dick got hard,
and
my eyes glazed "yes yes
YES!"
i didn't know i was gay
then. i'm assuming
he was straight.
he was sure beautiful,
though. the sight of
him naked in the
shower,
well,
the tip of his
dick,
so deliciously subtly
plum,

the twinkle in his
blue eyes,
the heart of the nation,
the
goal of loneliness quelchers
everywhere,
the taste of alcohol
not on his breath
and, back then,
never on mine.
**

these days, i like
alcohol quite a lot.
not that it fixes
everything.
not that that's what
i expect,
but,
hope springs eternal,
like
springtime flowers,
spewing their pollen,
as
sexy naked big-dicked teenage boys
look at photos of each other
and
spew their cum, too.
**

hip hip hurray.
the end of the world
is just a daydream
in the peatmoss
of bunnies,
nibbling their clovers,
as the sunshine turns
pretty much
everything a ghostly

shade of white.
**

nightfall. and
then,
the turtles
begin their
slow delirious fuck,
their eyes
shooting sparks
of
prehistorical
carthage, right
before the last of us
gives up his dreams.

petrol prices on the rise

the flowers that bloomed in the spring made
the sexy naked big-dicked teenage boy want to spurt cum.
the leaves that reddened and dropped in the autumn breezes
made
the sexy naked big-dicked teenage boy want to spurt cum.
standing alone in
the middle of the woods,
the sexy naked big-dicked teenage boy
smelled the air and
watched the birds
and listened to the clicky-clack trills of
mysterious hidden insects
and
it was there,
standing in the woods,
the sunlight warm and friendly on his broad sexy shoulders,
that
the sexy naked big-dicked teenage boy
tugged on his big hard throbbing dick
and
looked at the sky
and looked
at the
leaves vibrating at the tips of their
branches in
the mossy-scented breeze
and
and it was there that
the sexy naked big-dicked teenage boy
tugged on his big hard throbbing dick
and tugged gently and then tugged
some more
until
every cell in his body acknowledged
the certainty of
impending orgasm

and then
the sexy naked big-dicked teenage boy
spurted cum and spurted cum
and spurted cum
and
the breeze licked his tiny little
nipples
and
stimulated his tight pink little asshole
and
his cum plopped onto the ground
ten feet in front
of him
and the puddle
of
fresh cum dribbled from
that spot ten feet away
from him
all the way to a spot
right between his feet
as though it were a plume
shot from a fire extinguisher
and
it was then
that
the sexy naked big-dicked teenage boy
groaned and growled, almost a sob,
as
the birds sang and the insects
made their strange and mysterious
clicks and clacks
and the breeze moved the leaves
starting to turn
red in the fall,
the
flowers of spring
suddenly a sweet, sad, and strangely twisted
memory.

lotus maneuver

in the green mountains,
the sexy naked big-dicked teenage boys
walk around and spurt cum, onto the
loamy mossy ground, onto the tree trunks,
onto each other, and sometimes up each
other's tight pink tiny assholes.
oh yeah, up there in the green mountains,
the sexy naked big-dicked teenage boys
roam wild and free,
dicks up, hard-spurting cum,
eyes dancing with sparkly pleasure.
sometimes,
the sexy naked big-dicked teenage boys
kinda collide, as a group,
and enjoy the pleasures of each
other's company, all at once,
up in the green mountains,
the sunshine bright on
eager tawny skin,
all the sexy naked big-dicked teenage boys
that the green mountains have to offer,
embracing each other, for sex, and
warmth, and the
hot gentle vaguaries of
wet sloppy love.

knives, forks, and greasy old spoons

the sight of the silent dogs shook
him up, left him sad, drooling.
the dogs were usually so loud,
so boisterous. now, they
were silent. sitting
in the middle of the
street and brooding. their
tongues out, and
not even a drop of saliva
dripping.
**

the slinky sexy big-dicked young man
woke from this dream
sad, nervous, twitchy.
it was a dream he'd been
having a lot recently.
nearly every night, it
seemed. he didn't own
a dog. never had owned
a dog. didn't want
to own a dog.
didn't really like
dogs.
**

when talking with
his psychologist,
the slinky sexy big-dicked young man
said, "i'm still having
that dog dream, the one
where there's just a bunch
of dogs sitting around
in the street, and they
are very very quiet.
in the dream, i know that
they used to be loud
and boisterous,

but now, they're just
quiet. it's a real
sad-feeling kind of
dream. a real
downer of a dream."
the psychologist,
a 30-something attractive-enough
blond man,
says, "do you think you yourself
used to be happier, and more boisterous,
than you are now?"
"i guess so,"
replies the slinky sexy big-dicked young man.
"i'm out of college now, and my
job kinda sucks. i guess i was
a lot happier in college
than i am now."
"i see," says
the psychologist. "and what
did you do in college that
you're not doing now?" he asks
the slinky sexy big-dicked young man.
"i fell in love with every cute guy
i met," replies
the slinky sexy big-dicked young man.
"i was kind of always in love."
"and are you in love now?" asks
the psychologist.
"nope," says
the slinky sexy big-dicked young man.
"there's no one now."
and thus goes their
conversation.
the search for love.
the absence of it.
fears and hopes for the future.
**

that night,
the slinky sexy big-dicked young man
calls up a former boyfriend,
and they reminisce. the sex
had been good,
they'd enjoyed each other's
company. why not try again?
not much enthusiasm was
expressed.
**

that night,
the dream again,
the quiet dogs,
so silent,
the fur on their
faces
not even bothered
by the breeze.

fox grapes

"when tracing the veins on the dick of a
sexy naked big-dicked young man,"
says
the sexy naked big-dicked teenage boy,
"i like to use the tip of my tongue."
and, in fact,
the sexy naked big-dicked teenage boy
is saying this
to
a sexy naked big-dicked young man, while
gently licking that sexy young man's dick.
the sexy naked big-dicked young man is
a swimmer on the college swim team.
the sexy naked big-dicked teenage boy
is there for summer swim camp,
and
the sexy naked big-dicked young man
is his swim instructor.
one thing has led to another.
they are now both in the
bed of the
sexy naked big-dicked young man,
and
the sexy naked big-dicked teenage boy
is enthusiastically licking
the sexy young man's big hard thick throbbing dick.
"not that you have that many veins showing,"
said the sexy naked big-dicked teenage boy.
"as a matter of fact, you have
a beautiful dick."
"thanks," says
the sexy naked big-dicked young man
whose dick is being licked. "a little
more action now, okay?"
**

later, after they've both

spurted about half a gallon of
hot gooey cum each,
the sexy naked big-dicked teenage boy
is lying on top of the
sexy naked big-dicked young man.
they are chest-to-chest, face-to-face,
slimy dick to slimy dick,
balls cupping balls,
and the sexy naked big-dicked teenage boy
and
the sexy naked big-dicked young man
are gently kissing each
other on the lips.
"you taste like chlorine," they both
say at the exact same moment.
then, surprised by the exact convergence
of exact same verbalization at the exact same moment,
both the sexy naked big-dicked teenage boy
and the sexy naked big-dicked young man
giggle,
and
grin,
and
dream the dream
that all this lasts
forever.

lazy jelly beans and warm testicular praise

buttresses and frying pans
start the ball rolling.
then it's the skin game
of who takes off what first.
the gliding of the chipmunks
from toy story to toy story
only exacerbates the certainty
of dental elongation. the
oregano sauce on the best
pizza in town zippy
whets the appetite of
the sexy naked big-dicked
teenage boy
for the loftier regions of
masturbation, auto-stimulation
the choice at midnight,
morning, too, and noon,
just pretty much a-okay.
milk cartons full of the
sperm of a whole
bevy of sexy naked big-dicked
teenage boys
smell vaguely of sweet
surrender, mixed with
hot cider, and
just the touch
of an amorphous jot of
skittery and bourbon-scented
joy.

blame

when the meatloaf fell upon the table
and began walking around, the
sky was the prettiest shade
of blue for a picnic, the nicest
shade of blue you could ever
hope for.
all 8 of the sexy naked big-dicked teenage boys
sitting around that picnic table
stared at the meatloaf as it walked
amongst them.
these 8 sexy naked big-dicked teenage boys
had seen some remarkable things during
their lives, including the sight
of all 8 of them spurting cum
at the exact same moment as
they executed a really nice
art installation. still,
though, that walking meatloaf
took everyone by surprise.
"let's hit it with a hammer,"
said one
of the 8 sexy naked big-dicked teenage boys.
"we don't got a hammer," said
another of the 8 sexy naked big-dicked teenage boys.
"use the breadpan!" said yet another
of the 8 sexy naked big-dicked teenage boys.
and so, they smashed the meatloaf with
the breadpan.
the sky such a lovely shade of
blue; things like this weren't supposed
to happen on such a pretty day.
"this is just awful," said
one of the 8 sexy naked big-dicked teenage boys.
"who brings a meatloaf to a picnic anyway?"
said another
of the 8 sexy naked big-dicked teenage boys.
everyone looked around,
but no one stood up.

the luster of spartan teetotalers

during my life,
i have eaten a lot of shrimp, and i have
eaten a lot of fish, and
i like shrimp the best.
shrimp don't have any bones
to get caught in my mouth.
i hate fish bones in my mouth,
but, still, i keep on eating
fish, and hoping for the best.
eating fish usually turns out
okay. i like fish, and usually
i don't get any bones. but,
when i do happen to get
a bone, i swear off fish
for a while, and just stick with the
shrimp. shrimp are quite yummy,
and they sure don't have any bones.
**

this is the sort of conversation
that i, and most people,
have on a routine basis.
things that they share
with others.
food preferences. fish
and shrimp. reasons
for choosing between the two.
likes and dislikes.
things one avoids. and then
maybe goes back to.
**

chit-chat.
good ole-fashioned
friendly chit-chat.
shootin' the breeze.
**

things one talks about

with other people.
conversations one has
because one is conversing.
**

sharing.
**

i'm 61 years old now.
i recall that when i was
18 and a patient in
a mental hospital,
i was
on thorazine,
which i now know
is a major anti-psychotic
drug.
**

some folks'll say
just about anything they feel
like saying. it doesn't
matter what, and it
doesn't matter to
whom.
**

these people make me nervous.
and yet...
sometimes it's fascinating
being just close enough
to overhear what they
have to say.
and you know they'll say just
about anything.
**

once upon a time,
i was a sleek skinny
teenage boy lying naked on
a big smooth warm rock
in the middle of the woods,

tugging on my hard throbbing
purple-headed dick and spurting cum
under the warm nurturing
rays of the summertime sun.
i remember liking the smell of my own cum.
it was musky, male, and insistently
obtrusive.
i was happy
naked and spurting hot smelly
cum back when i was still only borderline
manic-depressive,
and at the tender age of
just 16.
**

these days i find it quite restful watching
goldfish as they swim in
big clear bubbling aquariums.
**

most everybody likes that.
**

don't you?

run that by me again

the crowd at the farmers market wanted fresh vegetables,
and lots of em— carrots, tomatoes, cucumbers, green beans,
squash, onions— and all kinds of fresh herbs, basil,
parsley, oregano, and fennel, and dill.
there was a lot of activity around one booth in
particular— a good-looking sexy big-dicked teenage boy
and his two parents were running that booth.
the teenage boy really was beyond beautiful,
right into the realm of the astonishingly gorgeous,
and pretty much everyone in the crowd
around that booth seemed to appreciate him,
and what he brought to the market.
the crowd at the farmers
market milled about, ebbed and flowed,
bought hundreds of pounds of fresh vegetables,
and at the end of the day the
good-looking sexy big-dicked teenage boy
and his two parents went home
along with all the others
who had set up booths
and sold vegetables.
a lot of people wondered
what the
good-looking sexy big-dicked teenage boy
did once he got home,
and those who thought they knew,
sweated a lot.

entry-level position

the need for proof is a funny thing.
we want to know. we want to be
absolutely sure.
**

for example,
the only way to be absolutely sure
that a sexy naked big-dicked teenage boy
has spurted his cum
is to watch him spurt that cum.
that means his dick needs to
be visible. not hidden.
but fully visible.
if we want proof that he's
spurted his load of cum,
we just need to watch
him spurt it, see that cum
squirting out of the
tip of his big throbbing
dick. further proof would
be touching that blob of cum with
our fingertips, holding
a droplet up to our
nose, confirming that
harsh musky sexual scent.
**

another example:
the only way to know
for sure
that the
eiffel tower exists
is to see it, and touch it.
photographs aren't enough.
photographs can be doctored.
**

i've seen and touched
the eiffel tower.

it exists.
but, does my word make
it so? or do you
need to see and touch
the effiel tower yourself? i think
absolute proof requires
more than my word.
or the words of others.
or those photographs
you can find anywhere.
**

listen, if you think
about stuff too much,
you'll go a little crazy.
**

trust me. (as the wind
howls outside your window,
and rattles the window panes—
rattles them, that is,
if those panes are really there.)

yellow gourds and pink gooseberries

"grassy growth rings of curvacious spleens" says
the sexy naked big-dicked teenage boy as he
is getting fucked by his best friend, tom.
the sexy naked big-dicked teenage boy is
svelte and skinny, whereas his best
friend and fucker tom is best
described as beefier, and more substantial.
"when the corn-on-the-cob is boiling in piping hot water,"
says the sexy naked big-dicked teenage boy,
"then the light bulbs on the kitchen ceiling sometimes
flash and pulse with pink-lipped electric fire!"
they are in the bedroom of
the sexy naked big-dicked teenage boy.
the sexy naked big-dicked teenage boy is flat
on his belly, and tom is on top of
the sexy naked big-dicked teenage boy,
tom's dick is deep inside the asshole
of the sexy naked big-dicked teenage boy,
and tom is
fucking the sexy naked big-dicked teenage boy's
sweet little pink asshole with
great precision and pure-tom-like enthusiasm.
"flights of fancy into outer space
are sometimes teeming with robotic jellyfish
swirling in the silent seas of strangers,
and friends, and relatives," says
the sexy naked big-dicked teenage boy.
tom keeps on fucking him.
tom is groaning and grunting with
lithe little animal sounds.
the sounds from the bedroom of
the sexy naked big-dicked teenage boy
are
rhythmic and ebb and flow and guttural
and whimsical and
between

the
odd enthusiastic verbalizations of
the sexy naked big-dicked teenage boy
and
the grunts and groans of big beefy
fucker tom,
there is the complexity
of simplicity,
the knowledge
of pump and push,
the
gush and goo and wet of
hot slivo-slimy ker-splash.
"good god keep the kleenexes by
the fireplace!" says
the sexy naked big-dicked teenage boy.
"right where i can reach them when
the world turns to ice."

a good day for a good day

gelatin on the tip of his tongue
made the sexy naked big-dicked teenage boy
smile. gelatin was so old-fashioned,
it wasn't even jello.
sometimes all it took to make
the sexy naked big-dicked teenage boy
happy was something old-fashioned,
and homey.
the gelatin didn't really have a flavor
that he could name, maybe beef broth,
but, well,
it just tasted old-fashioned,
and homey.
**
it was the first day of spring,
and,
after the sexy naked big-dicked teenage boy
swallowed all the
gelatin that was in the bowl,
he felt invigorated, suffused with
energy.
his big sturdy dick was sticking
up at the aesthetic slightly curved
angle that he
very much appreciated,
and,
when
he tugged on it for a while,
it spurted several big blobs of cum,
and the orgasm felt so
good he
nearly
bellowed like a bull,
but,
in reality,
he just sighed and groaned

a little,
he was so
well-behaved,
some day he'd make a very good
husband.
**

later,
the sexy naked big-dicked teenage boy
put on his clothes
and went to
the grocery store to
fetch carrots and ginger ale
for his mother.
it was still the first day
of spring, and
the soft pubic hair coiling
around his dick
had never felt
more friendly.

parmesan peninsula

the sound of tequila splashing in a glass,
what to mix it with, harsh cacti,
or cedric the magician?
**

the sexy naked big-dicked teenage boy
walks around in his apartment,
wondering what to mix his
tequila with.
the sexy naked big-dicked teenage boy
is very happy.
this is his first night in his
brand-new apartment.
his parents are paying the rent.
he has tequila, and mixing
decisions.
and his big thick dick is
hard as a rock, and he's
planning to drink tequila
and watch porn and jerk off
and remain
very very happy, perhaps
even achieve a higher level
of happiness than he
is currently enjoying at
this sexy sensuous
and tequila-scented moment.
**

so
the sexy naked big-dicked teenage boy
decides on the
basic margarita mix
and decides on "MIKE BLOWS BOTH TED AND WALT (AT
THE SAME TIME)"
and while
sitting on a nice soft towel
on his brand-new couch, sipping

tequila and margarita mix
and watching MIKE TED AND WALT porn
and tugging gently
on his own big throbbing dick,
his heart is beating strong sturdy
thumps of pitty-patty happiness
and when
he spurts cum
it goes all over his sexy naked
chest and sexy naked
belly
and he just
leaves it there,
watches it drip and
ooze a bit
as he
sips the booze
and watches
MIKE and TED and WALT
and
it's now 11 pm
and
the dogs of loneliness
are
no longer
panting outside his door.
they have given up,
and
are quietly licking
their balls,
adjusting to
the tune
of
joy.

operators are standing by

the crystalline nature of the power structure
means that the rat's nest of tricycle tires
will burn with a nasty-smelling smoke that
goes on for miles and miles. naked airplane
pilots, named mr bone and mr spike,
flying high in the sky, can
see the tricycle tire smoke, and smell it, too.
mr bone and mr spike don't like the
smell of that smoke, and
they fly their planes quickly
out of range. they sit there naked
in their separate planes.
mr bone and mr spike like flying
their planes naked, and wonder,
alone, if there are any other
pilots who fly naked. mr bone and
mr spike have never met each
other, but hope for the best.
**

down below,
a sexy naked big-dicked teenage boy
is trying to flush the tricycle tire smoke
out of his eyes with generous
quantities of whiskey.
his eyes are watering now,
and, he must admit, they
feel better. and so does he.
the sexy naked big-dicked teenage boy
drinks his whiskey,
and looks at the sky,
and tugs on his dick gently,
just revving up,
as mr bone and mr
spike, disappear on
the horizon.
**

a few minutes later,
when
the sexy naked big-dicked teenage boy
spurts cum,
the smoke has cleared,
the whiskey bottle is empty,
and
mr bone and mr spike have
consigned themselves to
lives of naked loneliness,
their dicks bouncing
along with the tired old thrill
of unexpected turbulence.

pubic hair and wine

like most children, jon and i go everywhere
together. we've lived together for over
30 years. jon is my lover. i refer
to him as "the sweetest man in the world"
and if that's not true, it might as
well be. he's securely at the very center of my
world, and that's for sure. i'm 60
years old. jon is 57. we were both
a lot cuter, and a lot sexier, when we
first met all those years ago
and fell in love and lust with
each other. now, the lust part
is a bit calmer, okay a lot calmer,
than it once was, but the love part
is just as stong. maybe even
stronger. we watch ourselves
getting older, we watch our
relatives getting older. some
of our relatives of course
have already died. jon and i think
about things now that we never
ever thought about when we
were in our twenties.
a sense of our own decline
is an undeniable presence.
a sense of our own approaching
old age. some would say
it's already arrived, at 60 and 57,
but wait until they hit
60 and 57, and i'll bet
they'll say that's not
old yet. but they'll
have the sense that
it's sure flirting with
being old.
anyhow, no one wants

to say that the best years
of one's life are already
done with. that the remaining
years are gonna be fraught
with surgeries and dietary
restrictions, and pills,
and blood pressure concerns,
but, well, since these
things are already happening,
it's difficult not to believe
that there won't be more
of that stuff ahead.
so, hopefully, jon and i will
cope, and drink our wine,
and love, and laugh,
and just hang in there.
for an indeterminate
amount of time. actually, it's sort
of like being in our twenties,
but nothing at all like
that. not even a teeny little bit.

Carl Miller Daniels lives in the United States of America. He's not a cowboy, but thinks about them a lot. He is the author of three chapbooks: *Museum Quality Orgasm* (1996, Future Tense Books); *Shy Boys at Home* (1999, Chiron Review Press); and *Riot Act* (2010, Chiron Review Press). *Saline* is Daniels' second full-length book of poetry. His first collection, *Gorilla Architecture*, was published by Interior Noise Press in 2011. He and his partner, Jon (aka "the sweetest man in the world"), have lived together for over 30 years.

The author gratefully acknowledges the following publications where many of these poems first appeared.

5AM Magazine

Asphodel Madness

Assaracus

BareBack Magazine

Chiron Review

Citizens for Decent Literature

The Commonline Journal

DNA Magazine

FUCK!

Gutter Eloquence Magazine

Last Train to Noir City

My Favorite Bullet

Nickel Steak

Rusty Truck

[sic] Magazine

Thieves Jargon

The Thorn Blog

Underground Voices Magazine

Zen Baby

Zygote in my Coffee

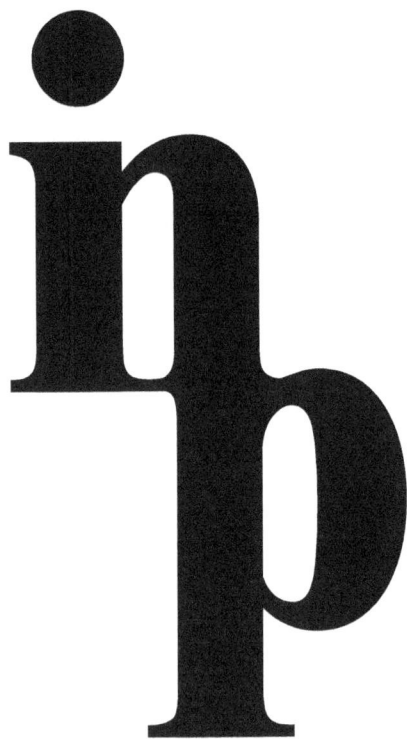

www.interiornoisepress.com